IPSWICH · FELIXSTOWE · WOODBRIDGE · MARTLESHAM HEATH
HADLEIGH · KESGRAVE · CLAYDON · CAPEL ST. MARY

AREA ROAD MAP pages 2·3
IPSWICH CITY CENTRE page 5
INDEX TO STREETS pages 27·32

AF470648

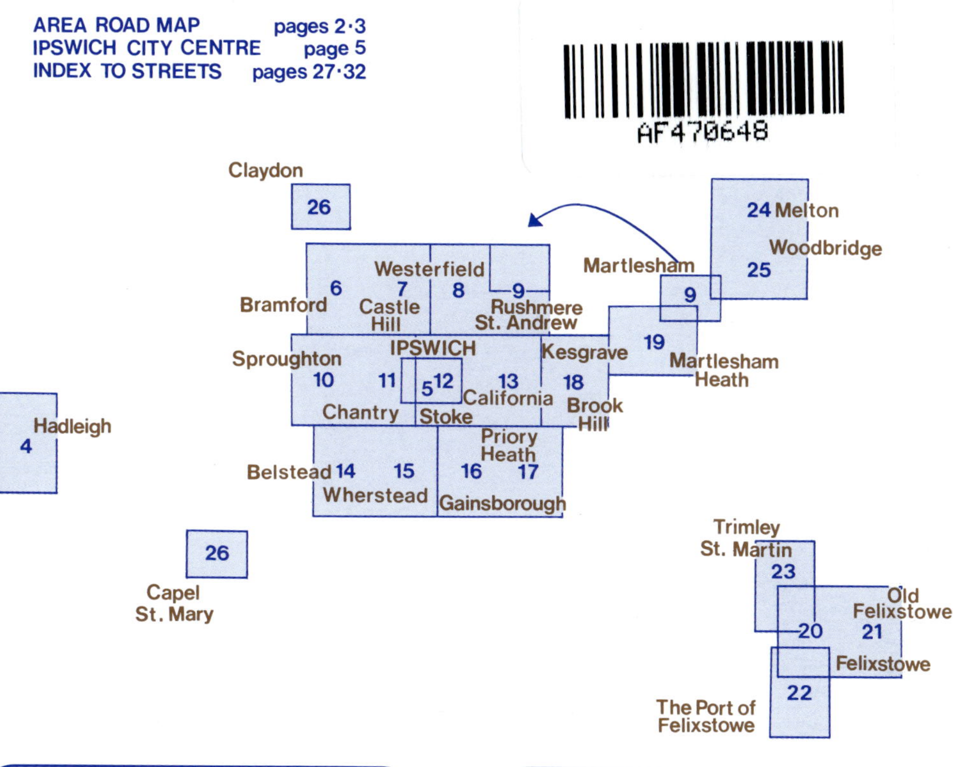

Every effort has been made to verify the accuracy of information in this book but the publishers cannot accept responsibility for expense or loss caused by an error or omission. Information that will be of assistance to the user of the maps will be welcomed.

The representation on these maps of a road, track or path is no evidence of the existence of a right of way.

Car Park	P
Public Convenience	C
Place of Worship	+
One-way Street	→
Pedestrianized	
Post Office	●

**Scale of street plans 4 inches to 1 mile
Unless otherwise stated**

Street plans prepared and published by ESTATE PUBLICATIONS, Bridewell House, TENTERDEN, KENT. The Publishers acknowledge the co-operation of the local authorities of towns represented in this atlas.

Ordnance Survey® This product includes mapping data licensed from Ordnance Survey® with the permission of the Controller of Her Majesty's Stationery Office.

Estate Publications 415 E   ISBN 1 84192 087 8

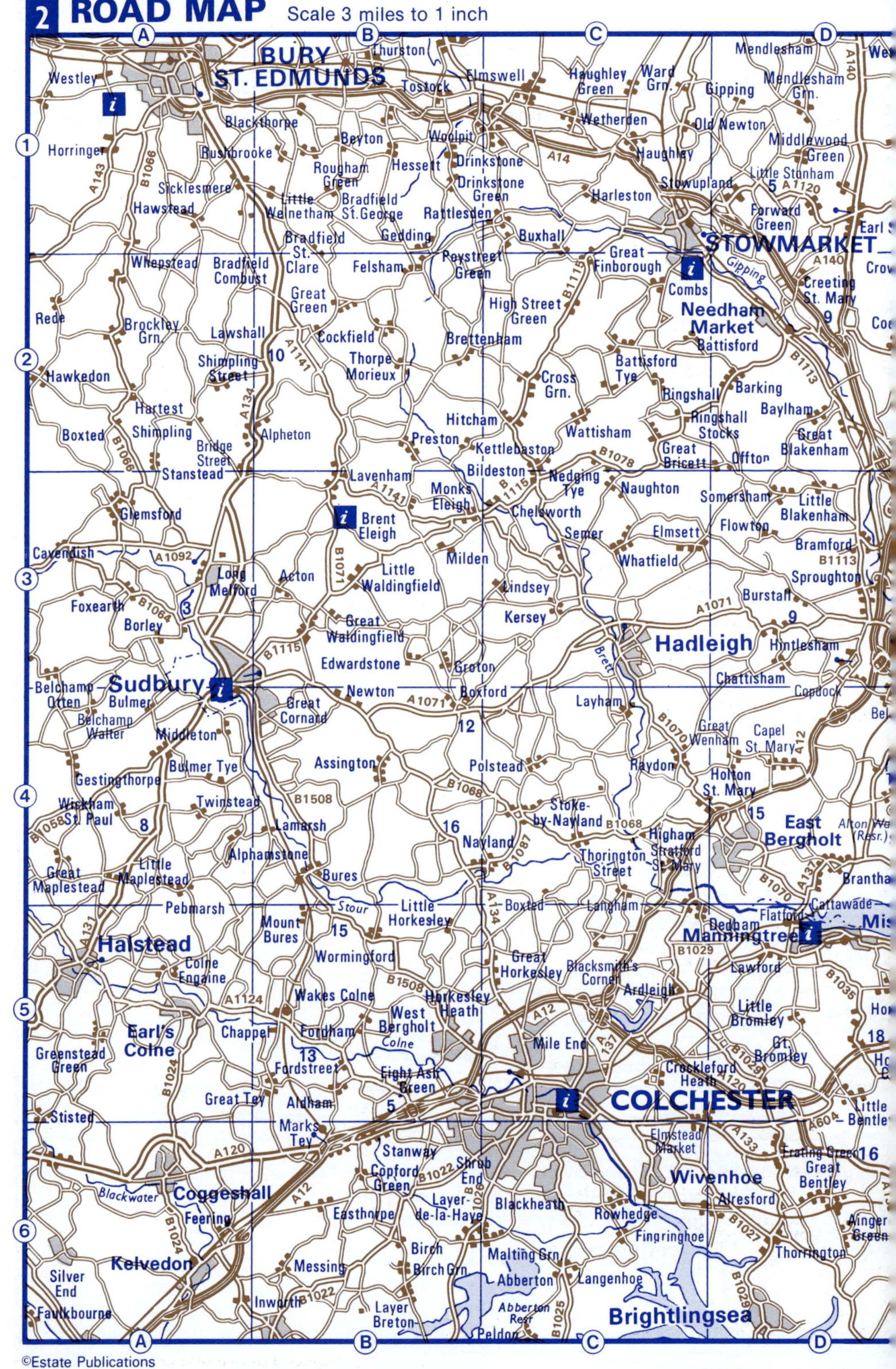
2
ROAD MAP
Scale 3 miles to 1 inch
BURY ST. EDMUNDS
STOWMARKET
Sudbury
Hadleigh
COLCHESTER
Halstead
Manningtree
Brightlingsea
Wivenhoe
Coggeshall
Kelvedon
Earl's Colne
East Bergholt
Needham Market
Mendlesham
Mendlesham Grn.
Gipping
Old Newton
Middlewood Green
Little Stonham
Forward Green
Stowupland
Haughley
Harleston
Wetherden
Ward Grn.
Haughley Green
Thurston
Tostock
Elmswell
Woolpit
Drinkstone
Drinkstone Green
Rattlesden
Buxhall
Beyton
Hessett
Rougham Green
Bradfield St. George
Gedding
Felsham
Peystreet Green
Great Finborough
Combs
Battisford
Battisford Tye
Ringshall
Ringshall Stocks
Barking
Baylham
High Street Green
Brettenham
Cross Grn.
Wattisham
Great Bricett
Offton
Great Blakenham
Blackthorpe
Bushbrooke
Little Welnetham
Bradfield St. Clare
Bradfield Combust
Great Green
Cockfield
Thorpe Morieux
Hitcham
Preston
Kettlebaston
Bildeston
Nedging Tye
Naughton
Somersham
Little Blakenham
Westley
Horringer
Sicklesmere
Hawstead
Whepstead
Rede
Brockley Grn.
Lawshall
Shimpling Street
Hawkedon
Hartest
Shimpling
Boxted
Bridge Street
Stanstead
Alpheton
Lavenham
Monks Eleigh
Chelsworth
Semer
Elmsett
Whatfield
Flowton
Bramford
Sproughton
Brent Eleigh
Milden
Lindsey
Kersey
Burstall
Hintlesham
Glemsford
Cavendish
Foxearth
Borley
Long Melford
Acton
Little Waldingfield
Great Waldingfield
Edwardstone
Groton
Newton
Boxford
Hadleigh
Chattisham
Copdock
Belchamp Otten
Bulmer
Belchamp Walter
Middleton
Bulmer Tye
Sudbury
Great Cornard
Assington
Polstead
Layham
Great Wenham
Capel St. Mary
Raydon
Holton St. Mary
Gestingthorpe
Wickham St. Paul
Twinstead
Lamarsh
Alphamstone
Bures
Nayland
Stoke-by-Nayland
East Bergholt
Great Maplestead
Little Maplestead
Pebmarsh
Mount Bures
Wormingford
Little Horkesley
Boxted
Langham
Thorington Street
Higham
Stratford St. Mary
Dedham
Manningtree
Lawford
Halstead
Colne Engaine
Wakes Colne
West Bergholt
Great Horkesley
Horkesley Heath
Blacksmith's Corner
Ardleigh
Little Bromley
Gt. Bromley
Earl's Colne
Chappel
Fordham
Mile End
Crockleford Heath
Greenstead Green
Fordstreet
Eight Ash Green
Colchester
Elmstead Market
Great Tey
Aldham
Marks Tey
Stisted
Stanway
Copford Green
Shrub End
Blackheath
Wivenhoe
Alresford
Great Bentley
Frating Green
Coggeshall
Feering
Easthorpe
Layer-de-la-Haye
Rowhedge
Fingringhoe
Silver End
Faulkbourne
Kelvedon
Messing
Inworth
Birch
Birch Grn.
Malting Grn.
Abberton
Langenhoe
Layer Breton
Peldon
Abberton Resr.
Brightlingsea
A143
A14
A140
A1120
A1113
A1078
A1115
A1141
A1134
A1092
A1071
A1066
A1064
A1115
A1508
A1508
A1068
A1087
A134
A131
A1124
A1022
A12
A120
A133
A137
A1070
A1029
A1035
A1027
A1025
A1029
A604
B1066
B1078
Stour
Blackwater
Colne
Brett
Gipping
©Estate Publications

3
E F G H
Kenton
Aspall
Saxtead
Monk
Soham
Brabling
Green
Cransford
Rendham
Carlton
Saxmundham
Debenham
Ashfield
Saxtead
Green
Framlingham
Sweffling
Sizewell
Earl Soham
B1119
Knodishall
Leiston
1
A1120
Brandeston
Great Glemham
Sternfield
Aldringham
Cretingham
Parham
Stratford
St. Andrew
Friston
B1121
Coldfair
Grn.
Thorpeness
Framsden
Kettleburgh
Hacheston
Farnham
B1068
B1122
Monewden
Hoo
Green
Easton
Little
Glemham
Snape
Snape St.
A1094
Charsfield
Letheringham
Marlesford
Campsey
Ash
Blaxhall
Aldeburgh
Otley
Dallinghoo
Wickham
Market
Iken
High
Street
Aldeburgh Bay
Ashbocking
Debach
Pettistree
B1078
B107
Tunstall
Tunstall
Forest
B1069
Marshland
Sudbourne
2
Swilland
Bredfield
B1069
Chillesford
Aldе
Witnesham
Burgh
Ufford
Butley
B1084
Orford
Grundisburgh
Hasketon
Melton
Eyke
Orford Ness
Bealings
Playford
Woodbridge
B1084
Rendlesham
Forest
Westerfield
Martlesham
Sutton
Boyton
Rushmere
St. Andrew
Waldringfield
Shottisham
Hollesley
3
IPSWICH
Kesgrave
A1214
B1083
Hollesley
Bay
Brightwell
Newbourn
Bucklesham
B1083
Alderton
Hemley
Ramsholt
Nacton
Levington
Kirton
Bawdsey
ORWELL
A14
Marshes
Chelmondiston
Trimley
St. Martin
Falkenham
4
Holbrook
B1456
Trimley
St. Mary
Walton
Harkstead
Shotley
FELIXSTOWE
Erwarton
Shotley
Gate
Port of
Felixstowe
STOUR
Wrabness
Parkeston
Harwich
Harbour
Ramsey
Dovercourt
HARWICH
Great
Oakley
Little
Oakley
B1414
5
Stone's
Green
HOOK OF HOLLAND
Beaumont
Hamford Water
Horsey I.
The Naze
ESBJERG
HAMBURG
CUXHAVEN
TURKU
Thorpe-
le-Soken
Kirby
le Soken
Walton
on the Naze
B1033
B1034
Kirby
Cross
6
Frinton on Sea
Great
Holland
B1032
Holland on Sea
E F G H
Reproduction prohibited without prior permission

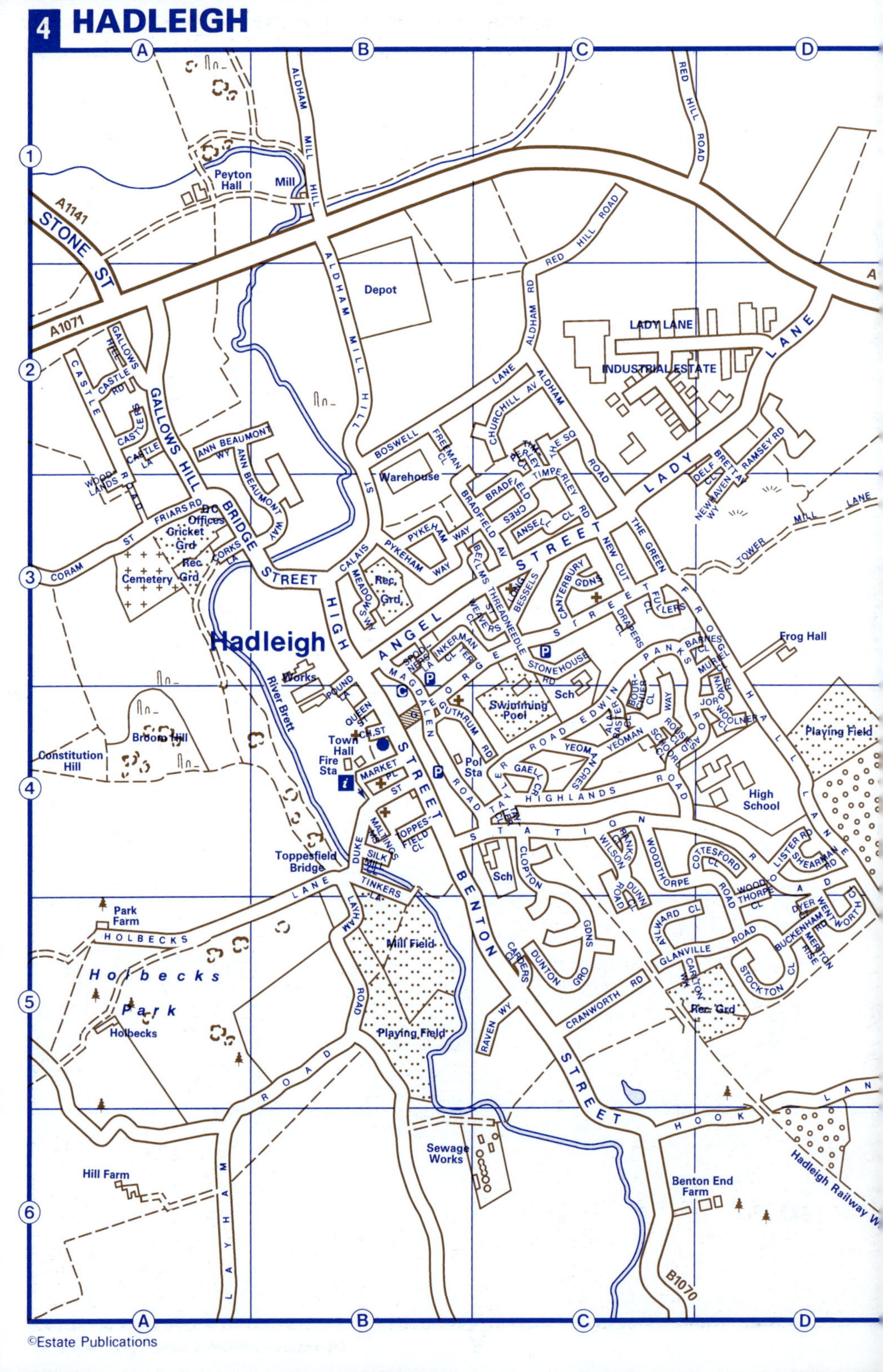

4 HADLEIGH
A B C D
1
2
3
4
5
6
A1141
STONE ST
A1071
Peyton Hall
Mill
ALDHAM MILL HILL
Depot
RED HILL ROAD
LADY LANE
LADY LANE INDUSTRIAL ESTATE
CASTLE RD
CASTLE LA
CASTLE ST
WOODLANDS
GALLOWS HILL
GALLOWS HILL ROAD
ANN BEAUMONT WY
ANN BEAUMONT WAY
FRIARS RD
DC Offices
Cricket Grd
CORAM ST
Cemetery
Rec Grd
CORKS LA
BRIDGE STREET
HIGH STREET
CALAIS MEADOWS WY
Hadleigh
River Brett
Works
Broom Hill
Constitution Hill
POUND LA
QUEEN ST
Town Hall
Fire Sta
i
CH. ST
MARKET PL
ST
MALTINGS
DUKE ST
SILK MILL CL
TINKERS LA
Toppesfield Bridge
LAYHAM LANE
BOSWELL ST
Warehouse
FREEMAN CL
PYKEHAM WAY
PYKEHAM WAY
Rec Grd
ANGEL STREET
MAGDALEN ST
SPOD NERO
INKERMAN CL
WEAVERS CL
THREADNEEDLE ST
ORG
GUTHRUM RD
Pol Sta
TOPPESFIELD CL
BENTON STREET
STATION ROAD
CHURCHILL AV
BRADFIELD CRES
BRADFIELD AV
TIMPERLEY
PERLEY
THE PERLEY
ANSELL CL
BELMS
LONG
BESSELS
CANTERBURY
STONEHOUSE RD
Sch
Swimming Pool
GDNS
ALDHAM RD
ALDHAM LANE
THE SQ
THE GREEN
FULLERS
DRAPERS CL
NEW CUT
ROAD EDWIN ROAD
YEOMAN
YEOMAN
GAEL CR
HIGHLANDS
TALER CL
STATION ROAD
TASTER YEASTER
BOUR-CHIER
SCHOOL ROAD
PANKS ROAD
BARNES CL
MURIEL JOR
WOOLNER CL
NEWHAVEN WY
DELF CL
BRETT CL
RAMSEY RD
TOWER MILL LANE
Frog Hall
Playing Field
High School
HALL LANE
Sch
CLOPTON
WILSON ROAD
DUNN
WOODTHORPE
PANKS ROAD
COTTESFORD CL
WOODTHORPE CL
GLANVILLE
CARLTON WY
STOCKTON CL
Rec Grd
LISTER RD
SHEARMAN RD
DYER WY
WENTWORTH CL
MERTON RSE
BUCKENHAM CL
Park Farm
HOLBECKS
Holbecks Park
Holbecks
Hill Farm
Mill Field
Playing Field
CARTERS
DUNTON GRO
CRANWORTH RD
RAVEN WY
GDNS
AYLWARD CL
Sewage Works
HOOK LANE
Benton End Farm
Hadleigh Railway W
B1070
©Estate Publications

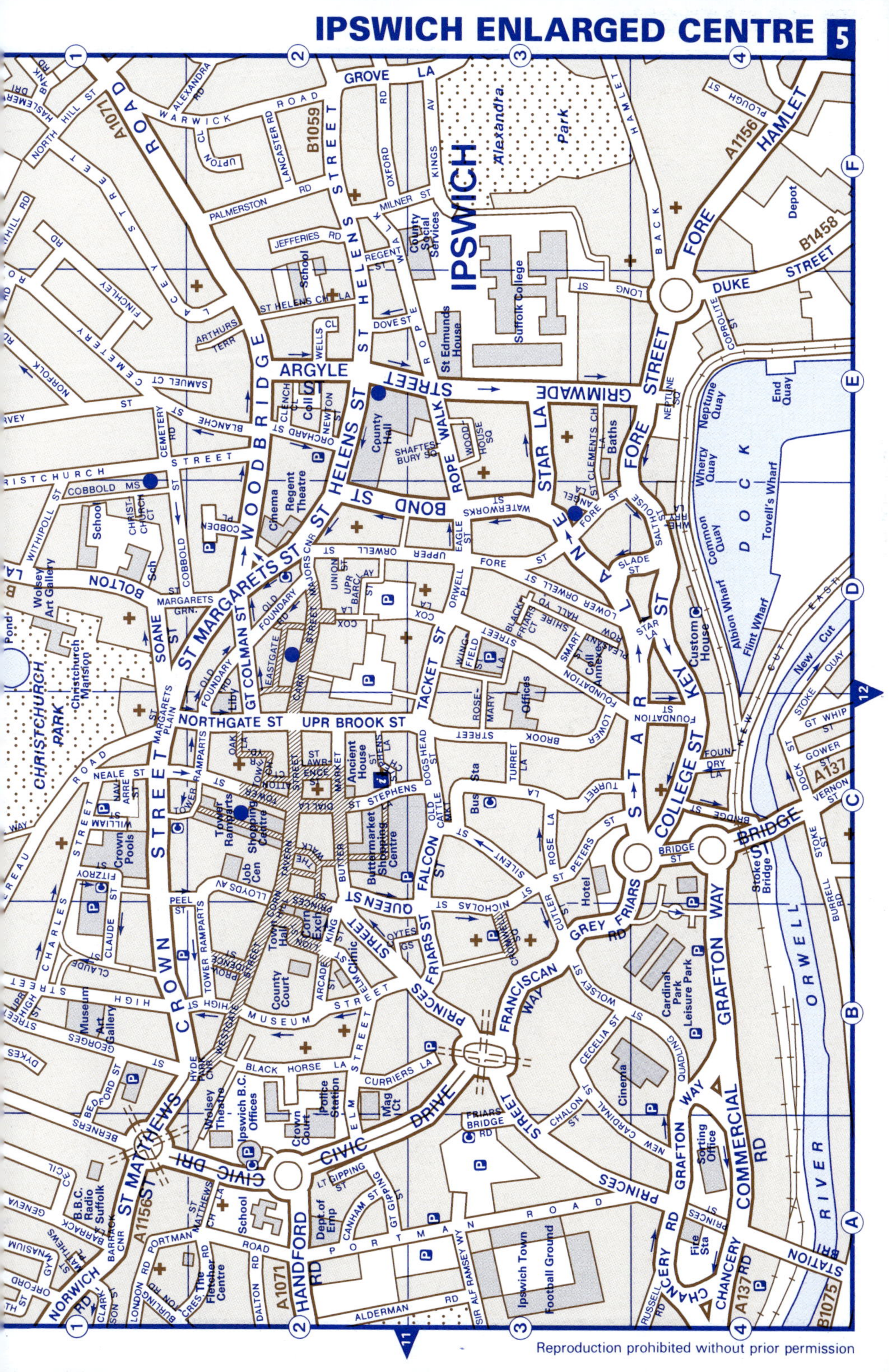
IPSWICH
Alexandra Park
Suffolk College
County Social Services
St Edmunds House
Regent Theatre
Cinema
County Hall
SHAFTESBURY SQ
WOOD HOUSE SQ
St Clements Ch
Baths
Neptune Sq
Wherry Quay
Common Quay
End Quay
Tovell's Wharf
DOCK
Albion Wharf
Flint Wharf
Custom House
New Cut
Regent Theatre
Wolsey Art Gallery
Christchurch Mansion
CHRISTCHURCH PARK
Pond
Crown Pools
Tower Ramparts Shopping Centre
Job Cen
Ancient House
Buttermarket Shopping Centre
Museum
Art Gallery
County Court
Corn Exchange
Town Hall
Clinic
Arcade
Wolsey Theatre
Ipswich B.C. Offices
Police Station
Crown Court
Mag Ct
Dept. of Emp
School
B.B.C. Radio Suffolk
Fletcher Centre
Bus Sta
Cardinal Park Leisure Park
Cinema
Sorting Office
Fire Sta
Ipswich Town Football Ground
RIVER ORWELL
GROVE LA
HASLEMERE DRI
BANK RD
NORTH HILL RD
ALEXANDRA RD
WARWICK
UPTON CL
PALMERSTON RD
JEFFERIES RD
LANCASTER RD
ROAD
B1059
OXFORD RD
MILNER ST
KINGS AV
REGENT
GRIMWADE
HAMLET
PLOUGH ST
A1156
FORE STREET
DUKE STREET
B1458
Depot
LONG ST
BACK
COPROLITE ST
WOODBRIDGE
ROAD
A1071
BANK RD
FINCHLEY RD
CEMETERY
NORFOLK LA
CEMETERY RD
BLANCHE ST
ARTHURS TERR
SAMUEL CT
CHRISTCHURCH
COBBOLD MS
CHRIST CHURCH CT
ARGYLE STREET
WELLS CL
ORCHARD ST
CLENCH ST
NEWTON RD
ST HELENS STREET
DOVE ST
ST HELENS CH LA
COBDEN PL
COBBOLD ST
SOANE STREET
ST MARGARETS ST
MARGARETS GRN
BOLTON LA
GT COLMAN ST
OLD FOUNDARY RD
EASTGATE
GARR
ST
FOUNDRY
MAJORS CNR
UNION ST
UPR BARCLAY
COX LA
ORWELL PL
UPPER ORWELL ST
LOWER ORWELL ST
ROPE WALK
BOND ST
STAR LANE
KEY STREET
COLLEGE ST
FORE ST
EAGLE ST
WATERWORKS ST
SALTHOUSE
WHERRY
ANGEL
SLADE ST
STAR LA
SMART ST
BLACKFRIARS
FRIARS
SHIRE HALL YD
FOUNDATION ST
NORTHGATE ST
UPR BROOK ST
TACKET ST
BROOK STREET
LOWER BROOK ST
STREET
ROSE MARY LA
TURRET LA
DOGS HEAD ST
OLD CATTLE MKT
ST PETERS ST
ROSE LA
SILENT ST
CUTLER ST
GREY FRIARS RD
FALCON ST
QUEEN ST
PRINCES STREET
FRIARS STREET
NICHOLAS ST
CROMWELL SQ
FRANCISCAN WAY
WOLSEY ST
CECILIA ST
CARDINAL ST
QUADLING ST
CHALON ST
NEW CARDINAL ST
GRAFTON WAY
COMMERCIAL RD
CHANCERY RD
RUSSELL RD
A137
STOKE ST
GOWER ST
VERNON ST
BURRELL RD
STOKE BRIDGE
BRIDGE STREET
BRIDGE WAY
STOKE QUAY
GT WHIP ST
DOCK ST
STREET
CROWN STREET
WILLIAM ST
FITZROY ST
CLAUDE ST
PEEL ST
LLOYDS AV
TOWER RAMPARTS
NEALE ST
NAVARRE ST
CURRIERS LA
BLACK HORSE LA
ELM STREET
KING ST
MUSEUM ST
WESTGATE ST
HIGH STREET
GEORGES ST
DYKES ST
BERNERS ST
BEDFORD ST
HYDE PARK CNR
ST MATTHEWS ST
CIVIC DRIVE
A1156
PORTMAN RD
HANDFORD RD
A1071
NORWICH RD
CLARKSON ST
LONDON RD
BURLINGTON RD
DALTON RD
CRES
PRINCES ROAD
CANHAM ST
GT GIPPING ST
LT GIPPING ST
PORTMANS WALK
ALDERMAN RD
SIR ALF RAMSEY WY
FRIARS BRIDGE RD
STATION ST
B1075
A137 RD
PRINCES ST

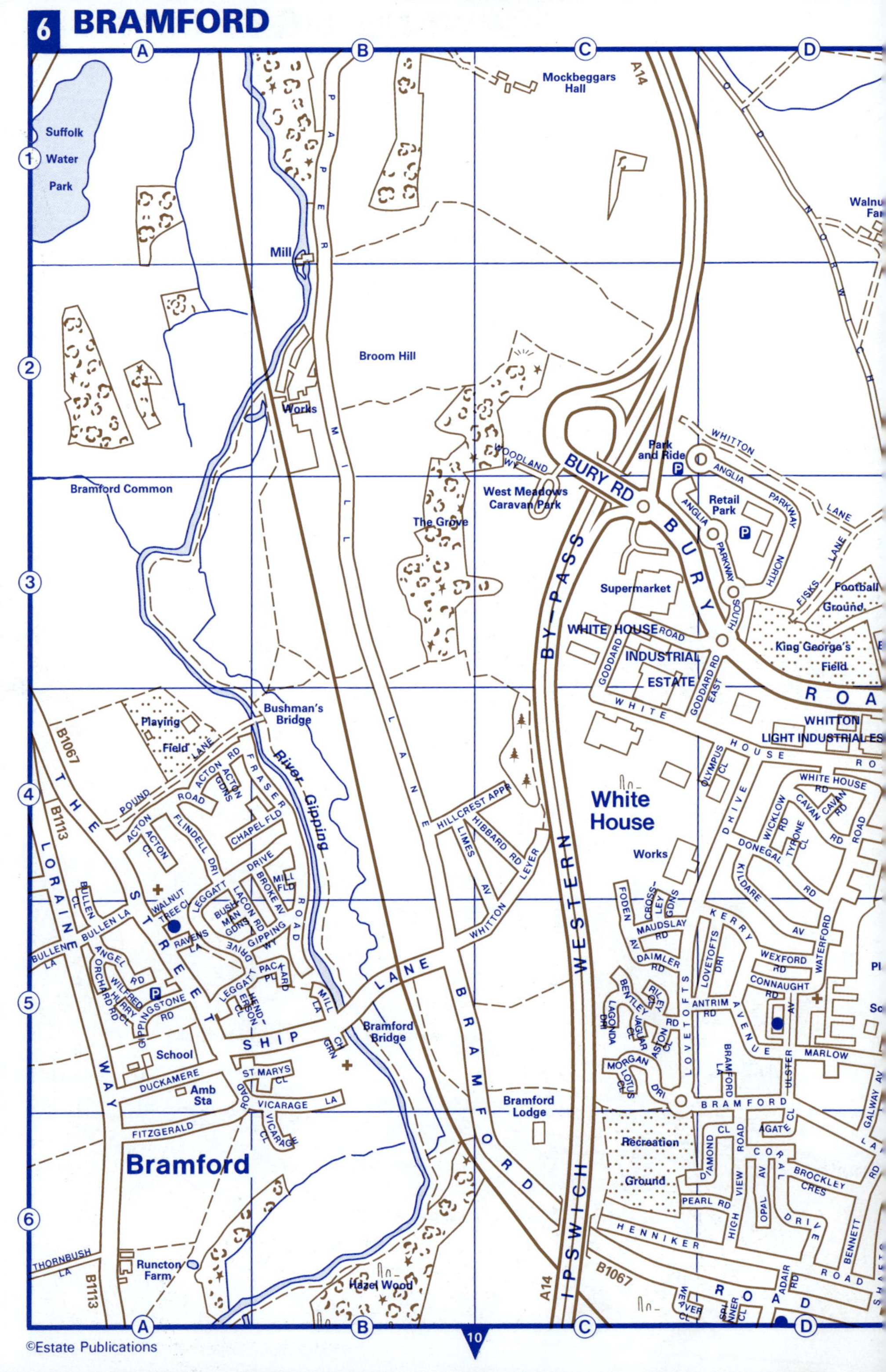
Suffolk Water Park
Mockbeggars Hall
A14
Walnut Farm
Mill
Broom Hill
Works
Woodland Wy
Bramford Common
West Meadows Caravan Park
BURY RD
Park and Ride
Anglia Parkway
Whitton
Anglia Parkway
The Grove
Retail Park
Anglia Parkway South
North
Fisks Lane
Walnut Lane
Football Ground
Supermarket
BURY
White House Road
Goddard Rd
Goddard Rd East
King George's Field
ROA
White House Industrial Estate
White House
Whitton Light Industrial Es
Olympus Cl
Drive
White House Rd
Wicklow Rd
Cavan Rd
Cavan Road
B1067
Playing Field
Bushman's Bridge
Acton Rd
Acton Gdns
Fraser Lane
River Gipping
Hillcrest App
Limes Av
Hibbard Rd
Leyer
Whitton
Donegal Rd
Tyrone Cl
Kildare
Waterford Av
B1113
The Lorain Way
Pound
Acton Road
Acton Cl
Flindell Dri
Chapel Fld
Drive
Broke Av
Mill Fld
Lacon Rd
Gipping Wy
White House
Works
Foden Av
Cross-ley Gdns
Maudslay Rd
Kerry
Lovetofts Dri
Wexford Rd
Connaught Rd
Marlow
Bullen Cl
Bullen La
Walnut Tree Cl
Leggatt
Bush man Gdns
Ravens La
Daimler Rd
Bentley
Jaguar
Riley Cl
Antrim Rd
Bramford La
Ulster Av
Bullen La
Angel Rd
Wilfred Rd
Gippingstone Rd
Leggatt Pl
Pac-kard
Hend-erson Cl
Mill La
Lagonda Dri
Morgan Cl
Lotus Dri
Lovetofts
Bramford
Avenue
Orchard Rd
Harry Rd
School
Ship Road
Ch Grn
Bramford Bridge
Bramford Lane
Bramford
Recreation Ground
D'amond Cl
Agate Cl
Coral Drive
Duckamere
Amb Sta
St Marys Cl
Vicarage La
Bramford Lodge
Pearl Rd
High View Av
Opal Av
Brockley Cres
Galway Av
Fitzgerald
Vicarage Cl
Bramford
Henniker
Bennett Road
Thornbush La
B1113
Runcton Farm
Hazel Wood
A14
B1067
Weaver
Adair Rd
Spinner Cl
ROAD
IPSWICH BY-PASS
WESTERN

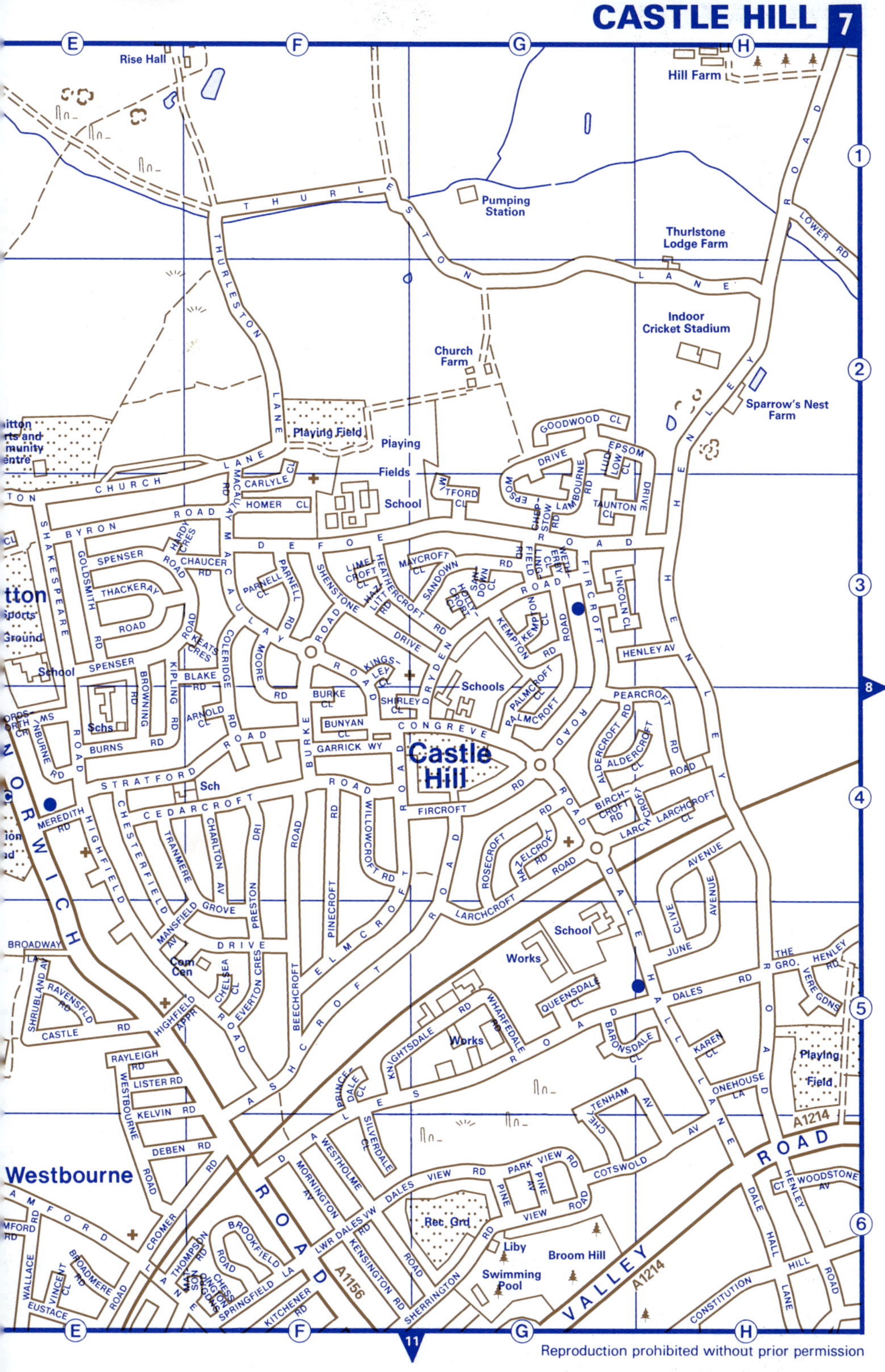
Rise Hall
Hill Farm
Pumping Station
Thurlstone Lodge Farm
Indoor Cricket Stadium
Sparrow's Nest Farm
Church Farm
THURLSTON LANE
LOWER RD
HENLEY LANE
Playing Field
Playing Fields
School
Goodwood Cl
Epsom Drive
Lambourne Rd
Taunton Cl
Chepstow Rd
Lincoln Cl
Henley Av
CHURCH ROAD
THURLESTON LANE
MACAULAY RD
Carlyle Cl
Homer Cl
Byron
Spenser
Goldsmith
Thackeray Road
Shakespeare
Chaucer Rd
Hardy Cres
Parnell Cl
Parnell Rd
Defoe
Shenstone Road
Lime Croft Cl
Heathercroft
Maycroft Cl
Sandown
Sann Down
Holt Croft
Kempton
Fircroft Road
Spenser
Kipling Rd
Keats Cres
Blake Rd
Arnold Cl
Browning Rd
Burns Rd
Moore
Coleridge Rd
Burke Cl
Kingsley Cl
Shirley Cl
Bunyan Cl
Dryden
Schools
Palmcroft Cl
Palmcroft
Pearcroft Rd
Aldercroft Rd
Aldercroft Cl
Norwich Road
Meredith Rd
Highfield Rd
Chesterfield
Tranmere
Charlton Av
Preston Dri
Stratford Road
Sch
Garrick Wy
Congreve
Castle Hill
Fircroft
Rosecroft Rd
Hazelcroft Rd
Birchcroft Rd
Larchcroft Cl
Larchcroft
Cedarcroft Road
Mansfield Av
Grove
Com Cen
Chelsea Cl
Everton Cres
Beechcroft
Pinecroft Rd
Elmcroft Rd
Willowcroft Rd
Larchcroft Road
School
Works
Clive Avenue
June
Avenue
Dales Rd
Karen Cl
The Gro
Henley Rd
Vere Gdns
Broadway La
Ravensfeld Rd
Shrubland Av
Highfield Appr
Castle Rd
Queensdale Cl
Baronsdale Cl
Cheltenham Av
Onehouse La
Playing Field
Rayleigh Rd
Lister Rd
Kelvin Rd
Deben Rd
Westbourne Road
Cromer Rd
Broadmere Rd
Knightsdale Rd
Prince Dale Cl
Silverdale Cl
Wharfedale Rd
Works
Cotswold Road
Woodstone Av
Henley Ct
Westbourne
Wallace
Vincent Cl
Eustace
Thompson Rd
Maxton Rd
Chessington Rd
Brookfield Road
Springfield La
Kitchener Rd
Kensington Rd
Mornington Av
Westholme Av
Lwr Dales Vw
Dales View Rd
Dales Vw
Sherrington Road
Park View Rd
Pine View Av
Pine View Road
Rec Grd
Liby
Broom Hill
Swimming Pool
VALLEY ROAD A1214
Constitution Hill
Dale Hall Lane
A1156
A1214
Kempton Road
Preston Drive
8
1
2
3
4
5
6

WESTERFIELD
B1077
Westerfield Hall Farm
Westerfield
FIELD
FULLERS
SWAN LA
ST MARYS WAY
CHURCH
MOSS LA
HENLEY ROAD
LOWER
ROAD
Mill Farm
ROAD
Works
WESTERFIELD
Millennium Cemetery
Sports Gr
Club House
Red House Farm
Playing Field
Playing Field
Playing Fields
WESTERFIELD ROAD
THE GRO
HENLEY RD
VERE GDNS
Playing Field
Playing Field
BROMESWELL ROAD
Playing Field
Northgate Sports Centre
Playing Field
CHELSWORTH AVENUE
DENHAM
DORSET CL
ELY RD
School
A1214
VALLEY RD
VALLEY ROAD COLCHESTER
SIDEGATE LANE WEST
ALMA CL
Cemetery
Fire Sta
HENLEY CT
WOODSTONE AV
THE
KINGSFIELD AV
BRETTENHAM
KETTLEBASTON WY
BILDESTON GS
CBBS
BORROWDALE
NORTH CL
SOUTH CL
TUDDENHAM AV
GROSVENOR CL
THE
ST ALBANS
CARLTON
WAY
ROAD
BERKELEY CL
Cemetery
CEMETERY LANE
BRUNSWICK
KINGSGATE
QUEENSGATE
CLARE RD
ROAD
DRIVE
LANCING AV
ELSMERE RD
AVENUE
ROAD
PARK
DALE HALL LA
PARK ROAD
MANOR RD
CONSTABLE RD
CORDER RD
PICTON AV

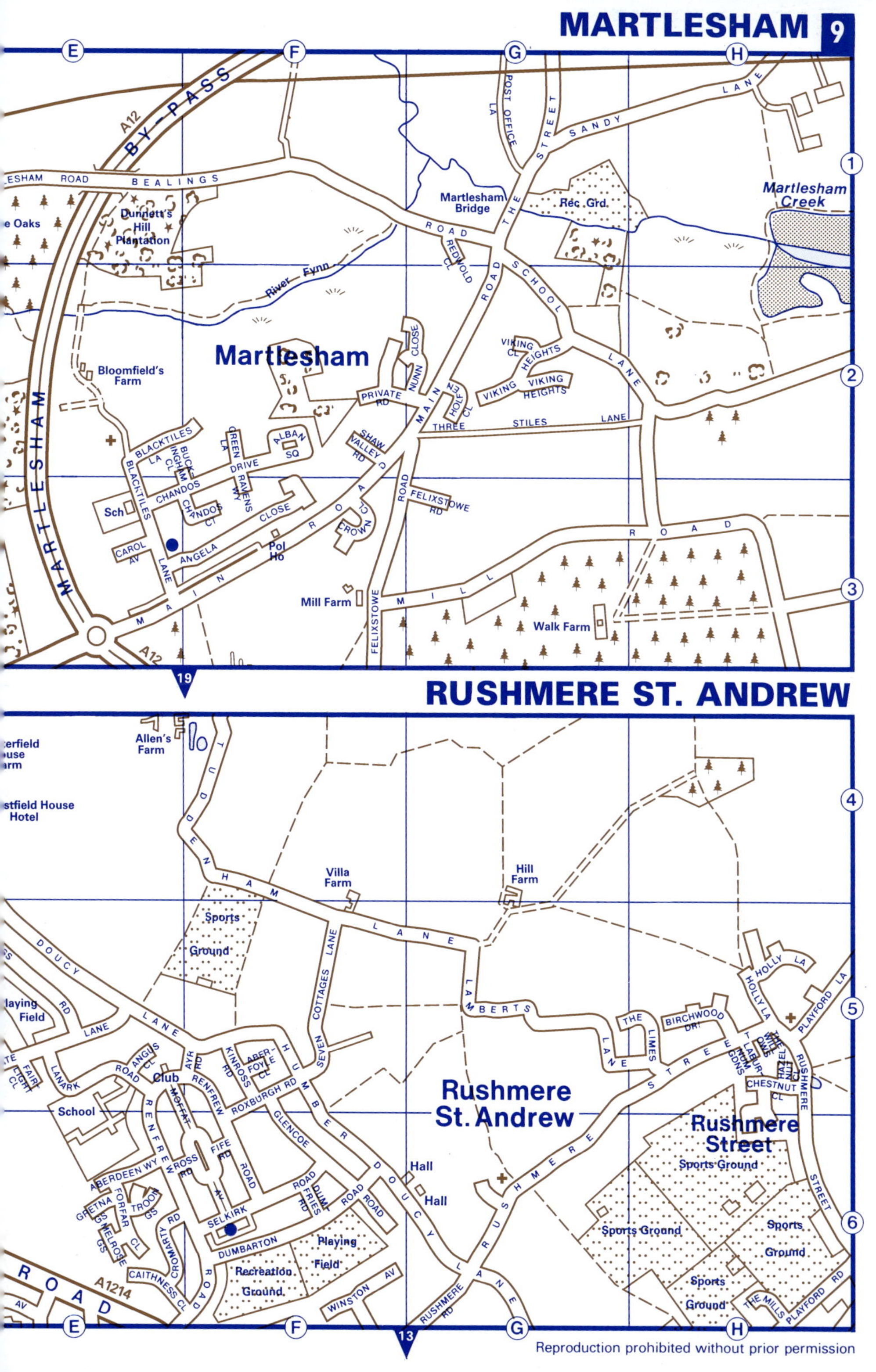
E
F
G
H
BY-PASS
A12
lesham ROAD
BEALINGS
e Oaks
Dunnett's Hill Plantation
River Fynn
Martlesham Bridge
Martlesham Creek
Réc. Grd.
1
MARTLESHAM ROAD
Bloomfield's Farm
Martlesham
POST OFFICE LA
THE STREET
SANDY LANE
REDWOLD CL
ROAD
SCHOOL LANE
PRIVATE RD
NUNN CLOSE
HOLT CL
VIKING CL
VIKING HEIGHTS
VIKING HEIGHTS
2
BLACKTILES LA
BUCK INGHAM CL
GREEN DRIVE
ALBAN SQ
SHAW VALLEY RD
RAVENS WY
MAIN
THREE STILES LANE
ROAD
BLACKTILES LA
CHANDOS CL
CHANDOS CL
CLOSE
CROWN
FELIXSTOWE RD
Sch
CAROL AV
ANGELA
LANE
Pol Ho
ROAD
ROAD
3
MARTLESHAM ROAD
Mill Farm
FELIXSTOWE
MILL
Walk Farm
A12
19

RUSHMERE ST. ANDREW
terfield House arm
Allen's Farm
TUDDENHAM
stfield House Hotel
Villa Farm
Hill Farm
4
DOUCY RD
LANE
Sports Ground
SEVEN COTTAGES LANE
HUMBER
LANE
LAMBERTS LANE
HOLLY LA
HOLLY LA
laying Field
LANE
ANGUS CL
HAYR RD
KINROSS RD
ABER FOYLE CL
ROXBURGH RD
THE LIMES
BIRCHWOOD DRI
STREET
RUSHMERE
PLAYFORD LA
5
ate
FAIRLIGHT CL
LANARK
Club
RENFREW RD
MOFFAT RD
RENFREW RD
GLENCOE ROAD
Rushmere St. Andrew
THE ELMS
TLABURT GDNS
CHESTNUT CL
School
ROSS RD
FIFE RD
SELKIRK
DUML FRIES RD
ROAD ROAD
Hall
Rushmere Street
Sports Ground
ABERDEEN WY
FORFAR CL
TROON GS
Hall
Sports Ground
Sports Ground
6
GRETNA GS
MELROSE GS
CAITHNESS CL
CROMARTY CL
DUMBARTON
SELKIRK
Playing Field
DOUCY LANE
RUSHMERE LANE
THE MILLS
PLAYFORD RD
ROAD
A1214
Recreation Ground
WINSTON AV
RUSHMERE RD
E
F
13
G
H

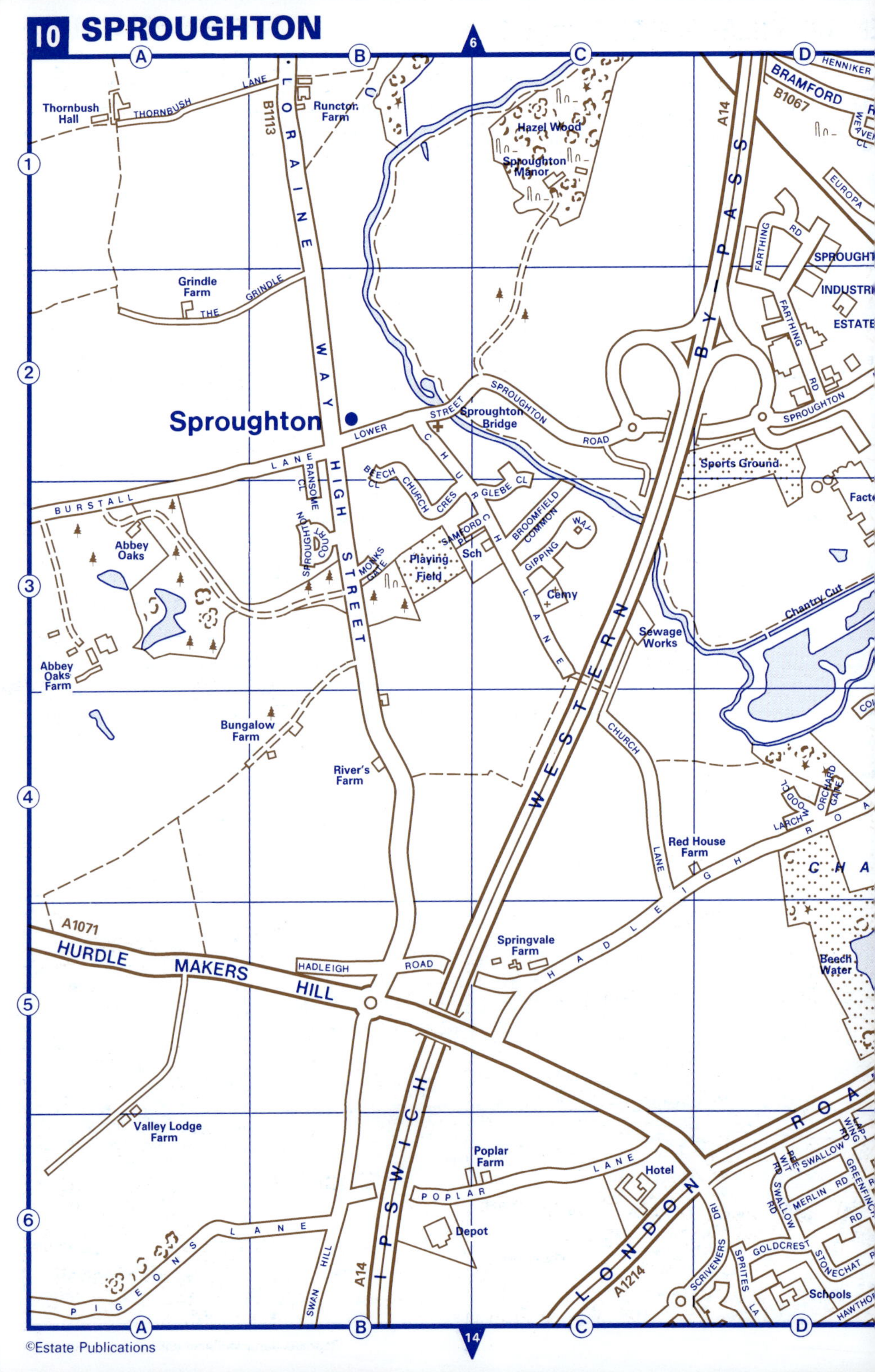
Thornbush Hall
THORNBUSH
Runcton Farm
Hazel Wood
Sproughton Manor
BRAMFORD
HENNIKER
B1067
WEAVER
CL
EUROPA
RD
FARTHING RD
SPROUGHT
INDUSTRI
ESTATE
FARTHING
RD
SPROUGHTON
LORAINE WAY
B1113
THE GRINDLE
Grindle Farm
BURSTALL
LANE
Sproughton
LOWER STREET
CHURCH STREET
Sproughton Bridge
SPROUGHTON ROAD
Sports Ground
Facto
RANSOME CL
SPROUGHTON COURT
BEECH CL
CHURCH CRES
GLEBE CL
BROOMFIELD COMMON
GIPPING
WAY
Abbey Oaks
HIGH STREET
MONKS GATE
SAMFORD PL
Sch
Playing Field
Cemy
Sewage Works
Chantry Cut
WESTERN BYPASS
A14
CHURCH LANE
Abbey Oaks Farm
Bungalow Farm
River's Farm
CHURCH LANE
ORCHARD GATE
WOOD CL
LARCH
C H A
Red House Farm
HADLEIGH
A1071
HURDLE MAKERS HILL
HADLEIGH ROAD
Springvale Farm
LANE
Beech Water
Valley Lodge Farm
IPSWICH
SWAN HILL
A14
POPLAR LANE
Poplar Farm
Hotel
Depot
LONDON ROAD
A1214
PIGEONS LANE
SCRIVENERS DRI
SPRITES LA
WIT
SWALLOW RD
SWALLOW
MERLIN RD
GOLDCREST
GREENFINC
STONECHAT
WING
HAWTHO
Schools

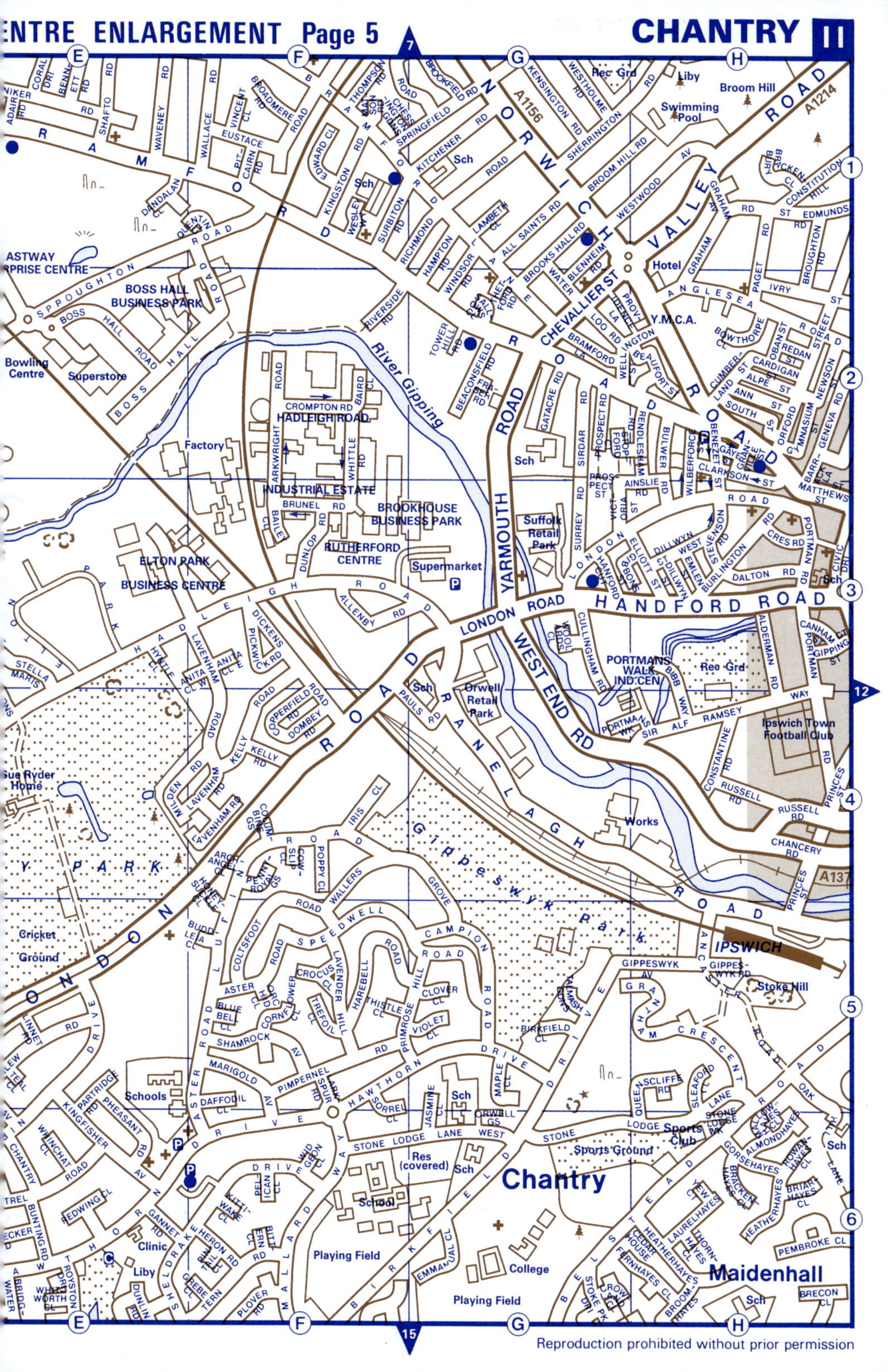

Broom Hill
Rec Grd
Liby
Swimming Pool
VALLEY ROAD
A1214
NORWICH ROAD
A1156
CHEVALLIER ST
Hotel
Y.M.C.A.
HANDFORD ROAD
LONDON ROAD
YARMOUTH ROAD
WEST END RD
River Gipping
BOSS HALL BUSINESS PARK
EASTWAY ENTERPRISE CENTRE
SPROUGHTON
Bowling Centre
Superstore
Factory
HADLEIGH ROAD INDUSTRIAL ESTATE
CROMPTON RD
BROOKHOUSE BUSINESS PARK
RUTHERFORD CENTRE
Supermarket
ELTON PARK BUSINESS CENTRE
Suffolk Retail Park
Sch
Orwell Retail Park
PORTMANS WALK IND.CEN
Rec Grd
Ipswich Town Football Club
Works
CHANCERY RD
RUSSELL RD
A137
Sue Ryder Home
PARK
Cricket Ground
IPSWICH
GIPPESWYK RD
Stoke Hill
Gippeswyk Park
Schools
Clinic
Liby
Playing Field
Res (covered)
School
Chantry
College
Playing Field
Sports Ground
Sports Club
Maidenhall
Sch
HANDFORD ROAD
PRINCES
BRECON CL
PEMBROKE CL

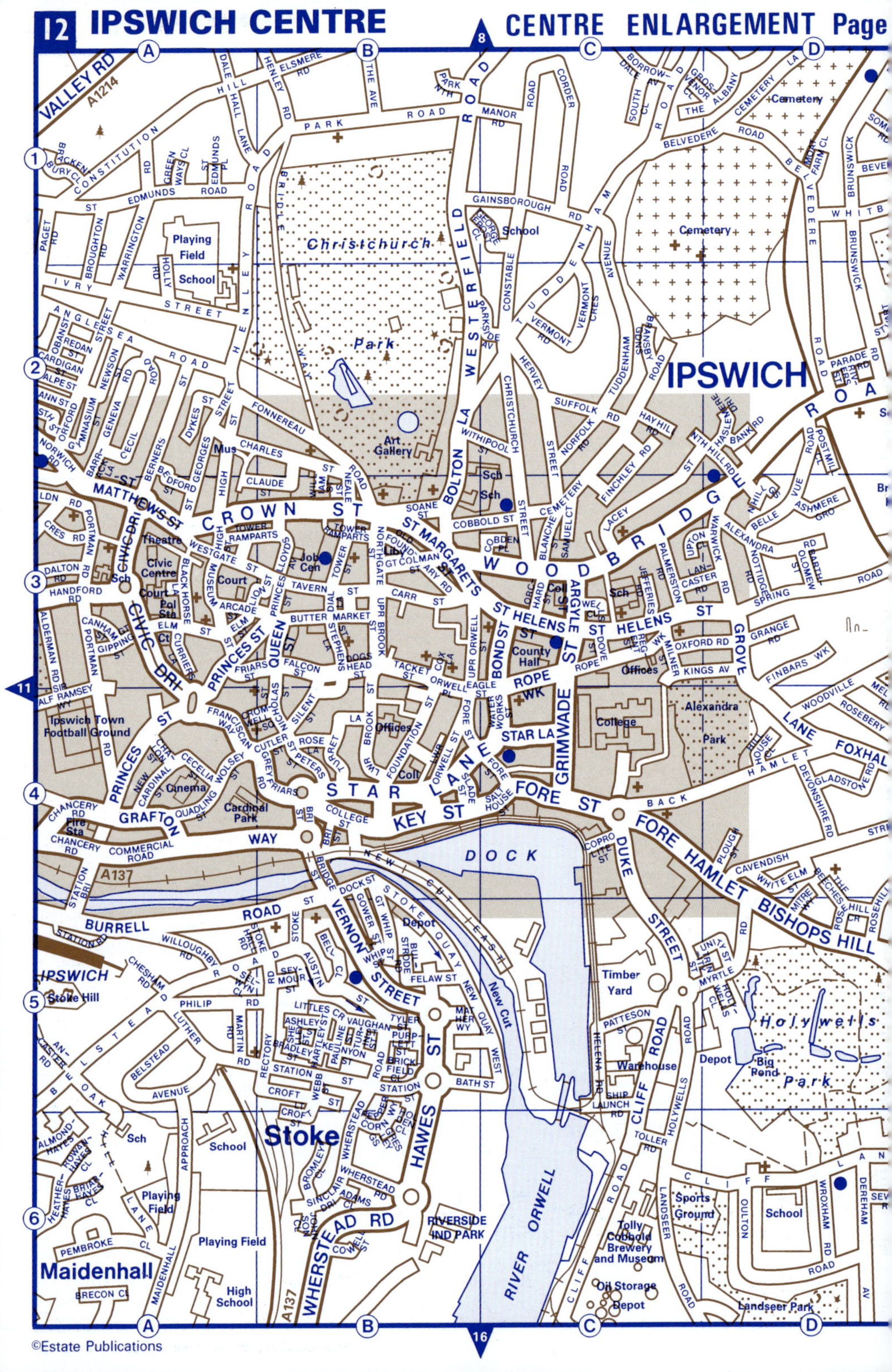
IPSWICH
Christchurch
Park
Art Gallery
Cemetery
Cemetery
School
VALLEY RD
A1214
Playing Field
School
Ipswich Town Football Ground
Civic Centre
Theatre
Museum
Tower Ramparts
County Hall
College
Alexandra Park
Cardinal Park
Cinema
Fire Sta
Pol Sta
Stoke Hill
Stoke
Maidenhall
High School
Playing Field
Playing Field
River Orwell
Dock
New Cut
Stoke Quay
Timber Yard
Warehouse
Depot
Big Pond
Holywells Park
Landseer Park
Sports Ground
Tolly Cobbold Brewery and Museum
Oil Storage Depot
School
Riverside Ind Park
MATTHEWS ST
CROWN ST
ST MARGARETS ST
WOODBRIDGE ROAD
WESTERFIELD ROAD
BOLTON LA
CONSTITUTION
HENLEY ROAD
BRIDLE WAY
PARK ROAD
MANOR RD
GAINSBOROUGH
CONSTABLE
VERMONT CRES
BELVEDERE ROAD
BRUNSWICK
PRINCES ST
QUEEN ST
CIVIC DRI
GRAFTON WAY
COMMERCIAL ROAD
BURRELL ROAD
A137
VERNON STREET
HAWES ST
WHERSTEAD RD
A137
STAR LANE
KEY ST
FORE ST
FORE HAMLET
BISHOPS HILL
CLIFF ROAD
DUKE STREET
GRIMWADE ST
HELENS ST
ST HELENS
BOND ST
ROPE WK
STAR LA
COLLEGE ST
GRIMWADE ST
GROVE LANE
FOXHAL
ST HELENS
ARGYLE ST
WARWICK
HANDFORD RD
ALDERMAN RD
PORTMAN RD
GIPPING
CHANCERY RD
CHANCERY RD
Offices
Offices
Butter Market
Dogs Head
Tower Ramparts
Job Cen
Court
Lloyds
Tavern
Black Horse
Court
Cardinal Park
Water Works
Palmerston Rd
Finchley Rd
Norfolk Rd
Suffolk Rd
Hervey St
Christchurch St
Cobbold St
Soane St
Fonnereau Road
Charles St
Berners St
Bedford St
Georges St
High St
Claude St
Withipool St
Park Rd
George St
Gt Colman St
St Mary's Rd
Carr St
Northgate St
Tacket St
Orwell Pl
Eagle St
Fore St
Cox La
Rope Wk
Milner St
Oxford Rd
Kings Av
Alexandra Rd
Nottidge Rd
Spring Rd
Grange Rd
Finbars Wk
Woodville Rd
Rosebery Rd
Devonshire Rd
Gladstone Rd
Back Hamlet
Cavendish
White Elm St
Rose Hill
Mitre
Beeches
Unity St
Myrtle Rd
Holywells Rd
Helena Rd
Patteson Rd
Toller Rd
Ship Launch Rd
Landseer Rd
Oulton Rd
Wroxham Rd
Dereham Av
Cliff Rd
Station St
Willoughby Rd
Stoke St
Bell Cl
Austin St
Seymour Rd
Whip St
Felaw St
Bath St
Luther Rd
Philip Rd
Martin Rd
Belstead Avenue
Anglesea Rd
Croft St
Rectory Rd
Bramford Rd
Pembroke Cl
Brecon Cl
Almond Hayes
Heather Hayes
Brian Hayes
Rowan Hayes
Maidenhall Approach
Sinclair Rd
Adams Rd
Bromley Rd
Wherstead Rd
New Cut West
Gower St
Gt Whip St
Stoke Bridge
Dock St
College St
Bridge St
Rose La
Foundation St
Fore St
Salthouse
Cliff Quay
Copro Cliff St
Plough Rd

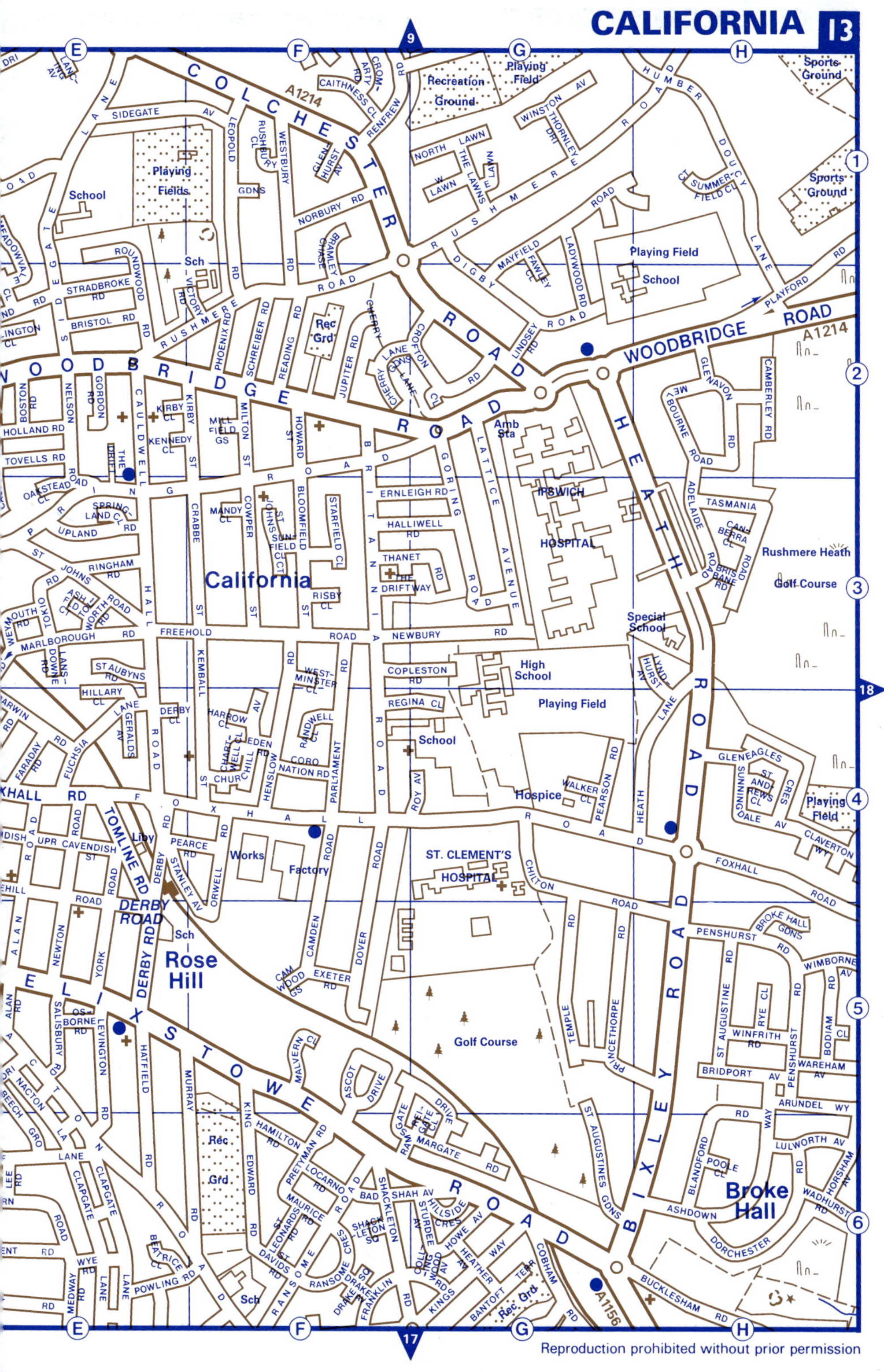

CALIFORNIA
13
9
17
18
1
2
3
4
5
6
E
F
G
H
COLCHESTER ROAD
A1214
WOODBRIDGE ROAD
A1214
Recreation Ground
Playing Field
Sports Ground
Sports Ground
Playing Field
School
Playing Fields
School
Sch
California
Rose Hill
Derby Road
Broke Hall
IPSWICH HOSPITAL
ST. CLEMENT'S HOSPITAL
Rushmere Heath Golf Course
Golf Course
High School
Special School
Hospice
Factory
Works
Amb Sta
Playing Field
HEATH ROAD
BIXLEY ROAD
Reproduction prohibited without prior permission

BELSTEAD
A14
IPSWICH WESTERN BY-PASS
LONDON RD A1214
LONDON ROAD
Park and Ride
Superstore
SCRIVENER
COTTINGHAM
OLDFIELD RD
DEVLIN
SOUTH GRO
WILDING
WARD RD
WILSON RD
GREEN SPIRE GRO
CHAMBERLAIN
CHERRY BLOSSOM CL
BROAD MEADOW
DRIVE
SHEPHERD DRI
WENTWORTH DRI
BEAN
COCK
HALL
MAGNOLIA
SKYLARK
Special School
BUTTERCUP
YEW TREE
SYCAMORE CL
RUDLANDS
BOWLAND DRI
KNITS
BALDRY CL
CURTISS
QUILTER DRI
ACER GRO
ADORN
FIR-TREE RD
SHORTLEY CL
PINMILL CL
WOOLVERSTONE CL
APPLEBY CL
SHORTLANDS
WARDLEY
SWINTON
LABURNUM CL
SPRITES LA
SPRITES
SCRIVENERS
BRAMBLE WOOD
BELMONT
MILNROW
MERRY MEET
WILMSLOW
School
STONECHAT RD
HAWTHORN
THE CHESTNUTS
RADCLIFFE
DIDSBURY
DENTON CL
HALE CL
ECCLES
CLIFTON WY
LETON DRI
BRAMHALL CL
ROAD
HOLCOMBE
BRIDGWATER
CRESCENT
MONTON RS
IRLAM RD
ATHERTON RD
EDGERTON
HEN-WOOD
ELLENBROOK ROAD
RITABROOK
COOKBROOK
TINABROOK
CAROLBROOK RD
ANNBROOK RD
School
Ellenbrook Open Space
Playing Field
Belstead Brook
BROOK
SWALLOW TAIL
SPECKLED WOOD
GROVE WK
MONARCH
GROVE HILL
GREEN OAK GLADE
OAK EGGAR CHA
BURNET CL
FORESTER CL
HOLLY
BLUE CL
WHITE
SKIPPER RD
TORTOISE
BRIMSTONE RD
ADMIRAL
GRAYLING CL
ELLENBROOK
MARBLED
CHESTER CL
DRIVE
WHITSWORTH CL
MIDDLETON CL
ROYSTON DRI
Stonelodge
Park
LAKESIDE
MANCHESTER
WORSLEY CL
DUNLIN RD
PLOVER ROAD
WOODCOCK RD
SANDPIPER
DAW BROOK
BIRKBROOK
BIRKFIELD
Liby
GREBE LA
CL TERN
KEEL
CAM DRI
ST CATHERI
Stonechat Rd
Hotel
A12
CHURCH LANE
Belstead Hall
BUCKS
HORNS LANE
Blacksmith's Corner
BENTLEY
LANE
THE STREET
CHAPEL LA
GROVE LA
HOLLY LA
HILL
Hall
Belstead
Alder Carr
Thorington Hall
Spinney Wood
Panning Hall
IPSWICH SOUTHERN
10

Chantry
College
Maidenhall
High School
Container Park
EMMANUEL CL
Playing Field
FITZWILLIAM DRI
CAMBRIDGE
MAGDALENE CL
School
SANDRINGHAM CL
DOWNING CL
HOLYROOD CL
BALMORAL DRI
GIRTON DRIVE
WIGMORE CL
PRITTLEWELL CL
LEICESTER CL
NEWARK
EGGLESTONE
DOWNSIDE CL
ALDERLEE
NETLEY CL
WINCHESTER WY
CANTERBURY CL
STAMFORD CL
BUTLEY CL
HALES CL
OWEN CL
OSYTH CL
FARNE CL
COOK CL
ROBIN CL
LINDISFARNE
GLASTONBURY CL
ABBOTSBURY
BLYTH CL
OAKLEE WAY
MESBURY ST
RAMSEY ROAD
WHITLAND CL
MALVERN
DAKLEE
WALTHAM CL
LANCEROS CL
FRITTON DRI
NEATH CL
STOKE
RIXHAM CL
HEXHAM CL
BUCKFAST
TINTERN CL
BROOM
CROWLAND CL
FERNHAYES CL
HEATHERHAYES
HAYES
School
BROOM
OKEVESHAM
MERE GDNS CL
CHESHAM
PRINCE OF WALES DRIVE
SAWSTON
TREY HEDINGHAM
CHATSWORTH CL
SPRINGHAM CL
HALIFAX
Supermarket
P
CARMARTHEN CL
MONTGOMERY RD
GLAMORGAN
CARDIFF AV
SWANSEA AV
TENBY ROAD
MONMOUTH CL
BRECON CL
SNOW CL
BLETCH CL
FLINT CL
MAIDENHALL APPR
MAIDENHALL GRN
CONWAY CL
FLINT CL
Sports Centre
A137
WHERSTEAD ROAD
Container Park
West Bank Ferry Terminal
RIVER ORWELL
Stoke Park Shopping Centre
P
Spinney Covert
Sports Ground
Caravan Park
BOSTOCK RD
Caravan Park
Bourne Park
AVENUE
Stoke Park CORPORATION
Fishpond Covert
THE HILL
Oyster Reach P.H.
THE STRAND
B1456
Ashground Plantation
Sewage Works
LA
BOBBITS
Camp Yard
Ski Slope
Bourne Hill
BOURNE
Sandpit Covert
LANE
Chapman's Grove
Home Covert
A14
SOUTHERN BY-PASS
IPSWICH
BY PASS
Broomhaughton Covert
Covert
Wherstead Park
Sports Ground
Wherstead Hall
THE STREET
Wherstead
A137
Icehouse Covert
Fish Pond
VICARAGE LANE
REDGATE LANE

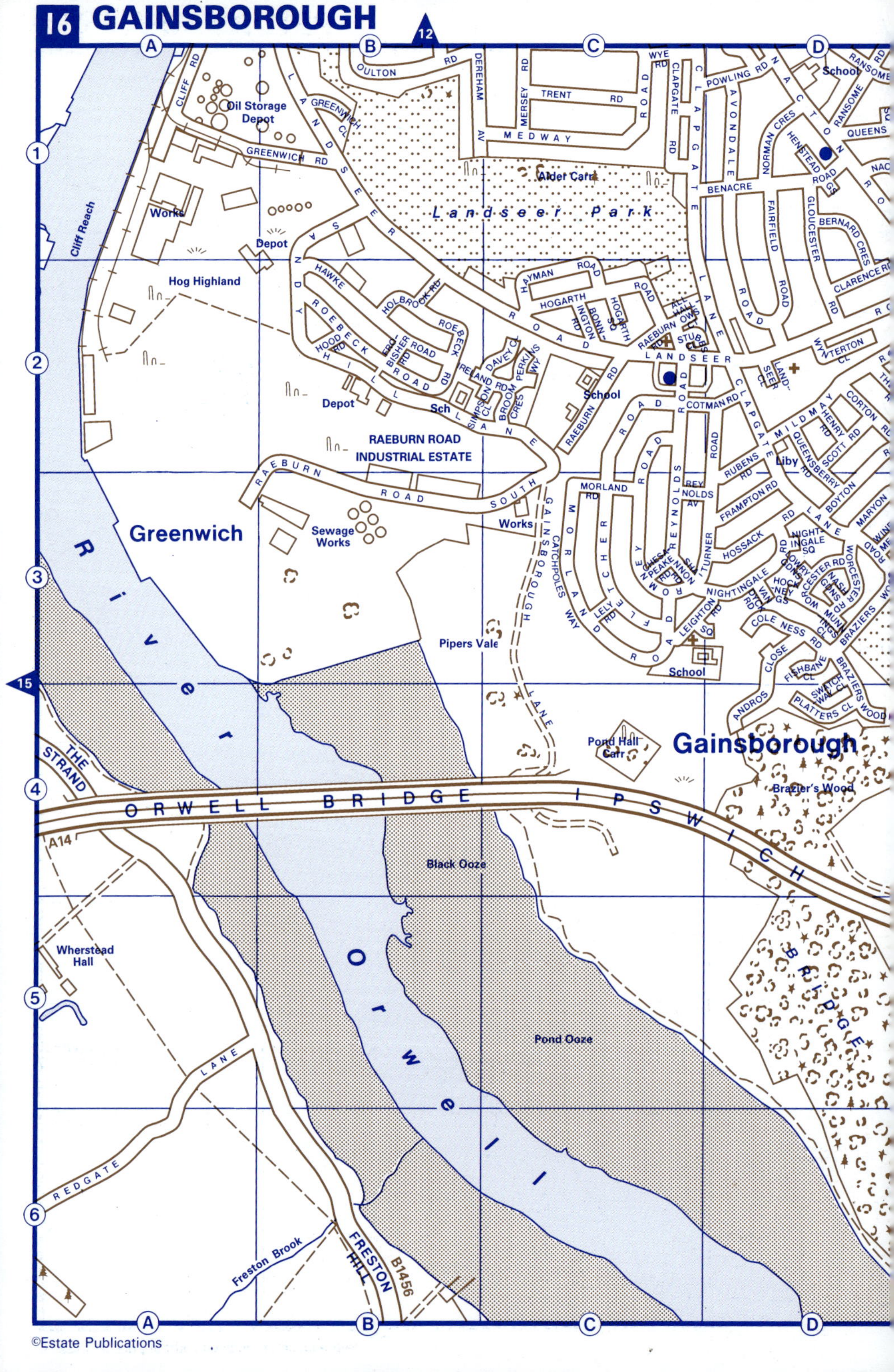

©Estate Publications

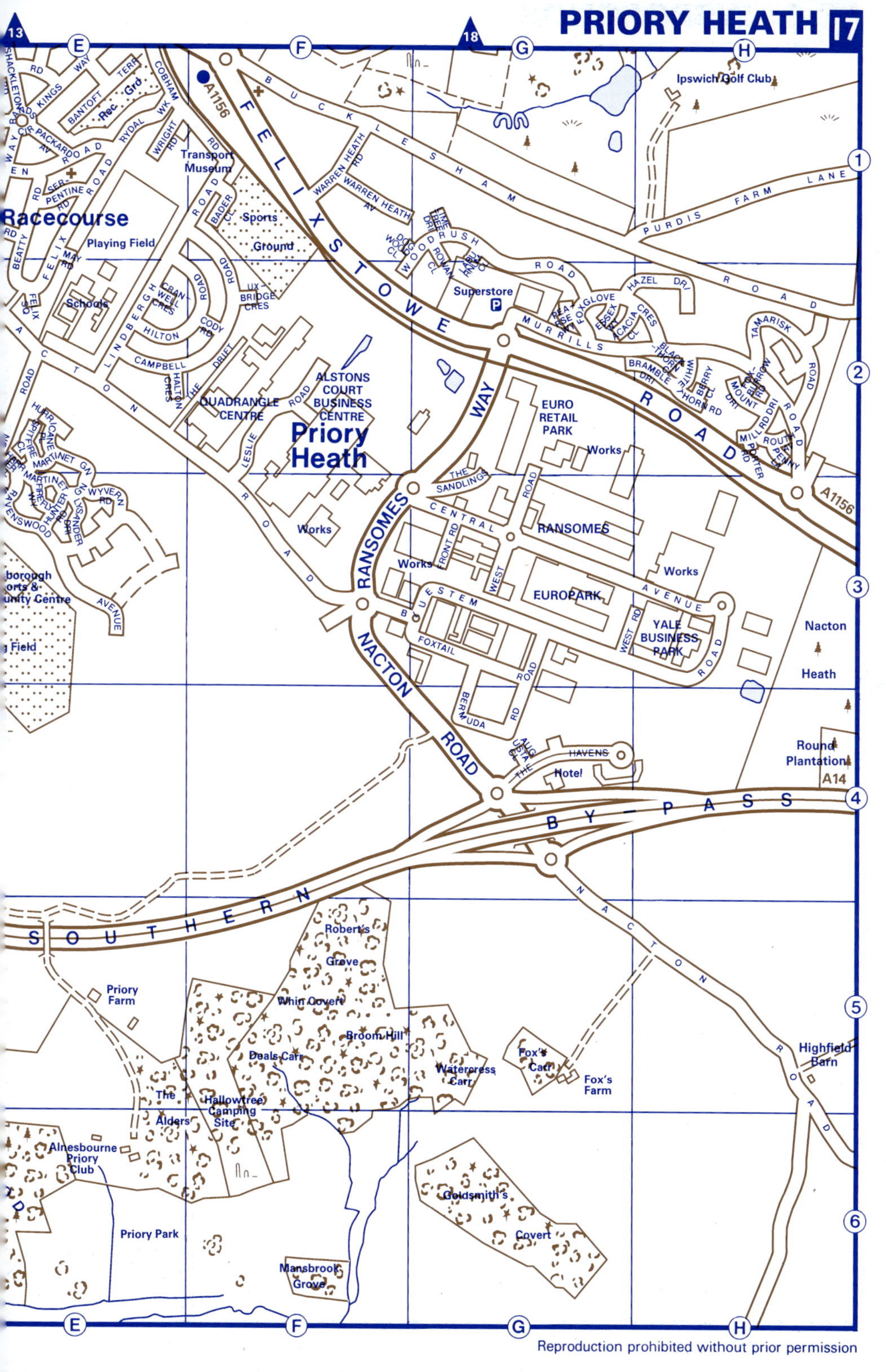
PRIORY HEATH
13
18
E
F
G
H
Ipswich Golf Club
SHACKLETONS RD
KINGS WAY
BANTOFT
TERR
COBHAM WK
WRIGHT RD
Rec. Grd.
PACKARD ROAD
RYDAL
A1156
Transport Museum
FELIXSTOWE
BUCKLESHAM ROAD
WARREN HEATH RD
WARREN HEATH AV
PURDIS FARM LANE
1
Racecourse
BEATTY
FELIX RD
MAY RD
Playing Field
Sports Ground
BADER CL
CODY RD
THE DUET
CRAN WELL CRES
HILTON
CAMPBELL CRES
HALTON
LINDBERGH ROAD
UX BRIDGE CRES
DOGWOOD CL
ROWAN CL
LIME TREE DRI
THE BRUSH
Superstore
P
ROAD
MURRILLS
PEARTREE WY
FOXGLOVE CL
ESSEX CL
ACACIA CRES
HAZEL DRI
BLACKTHORN
WHITETHORN
BRAMBLE DRI
BERRY CL
FOX BURROW
MILL RD DRI
TAMARISK ROAD
PENNY LA
ROUTH
PORTER
2
ACTON ROAD
HURRICANE
SPITFIRE RD
MARTINET
MARTINET GN
RAVENSWOOD
WYVERN RD
LYSANDER DRI
FURY
HUNTER
AVENUE
QUADRANGLE CENTRE
LESLIE ROAD
ALSTONS COURT BUSINESS CENTRE
Priory Heath
EURO RETAIL PARK
Works
ROAD
A1156
borough Sports & unity Centre
Works
RANSOMES WAY
THE SANDLINGS
CENTRAL RD
FRONT RD
WEST RD
RANSOMES
EUROPARK
Works
AVENUE
Nacton
3
g Field
NACTON ROAD
BLUE STEM
FOXTAIL
BERMUDA RD
WEST RD
YALE BUSINESS PARK
ROAD
Heath
Round Plantation
A14
AUGUSTA
THE HAVENS
Hotel
4
BY - PASS
NACTON ROAD
SOUTHERN
Robert's Grove
Priory Farm
Whin Covert
Broom Hill
Deals Carr
Watercress Carr
Fox's Carr
Fox's Farm
5
Highfield Barn
The Alders
Hallowtree Camping Site
Alnesbourne Priory Club
Goldsmith's Covert
6
Priory Park
Mansbrook Grove
E
F
G
H

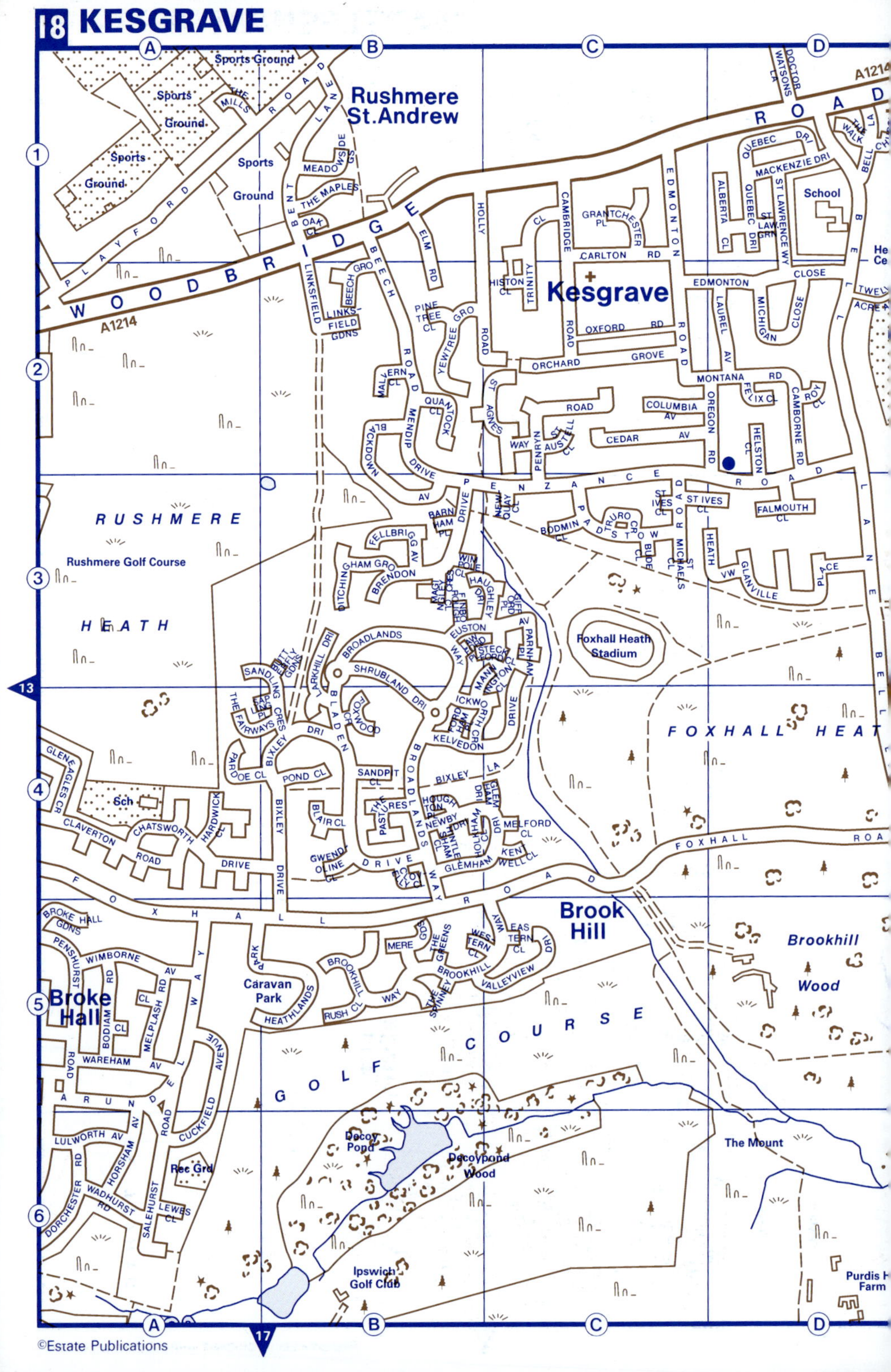

Sports Ground
Sports Ground
Sports Ground
Sports Ground
THE MILLS
Rushmere St.Andrew
PLAYFORD ROAD
THE ROAD
MEADOWSIDE
BENT LANE
THE MAPLES
OAT
LINKSFIELD
BEECH GRO
ELM RD
BEECH
LINKS FIELD GDNS
WOODBRIDGE
A1214
WOODBRIDGE
A1214
HOLLY
CAMBRIDGE CL
GRANTCHESTER PL
EDMONTON
QUEBEC DRI
MACKENZIE DRI
ALBERTA CL
QUEBEC DRI
ST LAWRENCE WY
ST LAW GRN
School
THE WALK
BELL LA
CARLTON RD
DOCTOR WATSONS LA
A1214
ROAD
He
Ce
PINE TREE CL
YEWTREE GRO
HISTON CL
TRINITY
Kesgrave
EDMONTON
LAUREL AV
MICHIGAN
CLOSE
TWELV
ACRE
MALVERN CL
MENDIP DRIVE
QUANTOCK CL
ROAD
ST AGNES
ROAD
OXFORD RD
ORCHARD
GROVE
MONTANA RD
FELIX CL
ROC
CAMBORNE RD
BLACKDOWN AV
NEW QUAY CL
WAY
PENRYN
ST AUSTELL CL
ROAD
CEDAR
COLUMBIA AV
OREGON RD
HELSTON CL
FALMOUTH CL
RUSHMERE
Rushmere Golf Course
HEATH
BARNHAM PL
PENZANCE
BODMIN
PADSTOW
TRURO
CROW
ST IVES CL
ST IVES
ST MICHAELS
GLANVILLE
VW
HEATH
PLACE
FELLBRIGG AV
DITCHINGHAM GRO
BRENDON
HAUGHLEY DRI
WINPOLE CL
EUSTON WAY
PARNHAM DRIVE
Foxhall Heath Stadium
FOXHALL HEATH
BROADLANDS
SANDLING
LARKHILL DRI
BLADEN
SHRUBLAND DRI
ICKWORTH CR
KELVEDON
MAINGRO
WINGTON CL
STECKFORD
THE FAIRWAYS
BIXLEY CL
PARDOE CL
POND CL
FOXWOOD DRI
SANDPIT CL
BIXLEY LA
BROADLANDS
GLEMHAM DRI
HOUGHTON PL
THE PASTURES
NEWBY
BIXLEY DRIVE
BLAIR CL
GWENDOLINE CE
FOXY CL
GLEMHAM WAY
INTLESHAM
MELFORD CL
KENT WELL CL
FOXHALL ROAD
FOXHALL
ROA
GLENEAGLES CR
Sch
CLAVERTON ROAD
CHATSWORTH
HARDWICK CL
DRIVE
FOXHALL WAY
Brook Hill
Brookhill Wood
BROKE HALL GDNS
PENSHURST
WIMBORNE RD
BODIAM CL
MELPLASH RD
PARK
MERE GDNS
BROOKHILL WAY
THE GREENS
WESTERN CL
EASTERN CL
VALLEYVIEW DRI
THE SANNEY WAY
Broke Hall
WAREHAM AV
ARUNDEL ROAD
Caravan Park
HEATHLANDS
RUSH CL
BROOKHILL WAY
GOLF COURSE
LULWORTH AV
HORSHAM AV
WADHURST RD
DORCHESTER RD
SALEHURST
LEWES CL
CUCKFIELD ROAD
Rec Grd
Decoy Pond
Decoypond Wood
The Mount
Purdis H Farm
Ipswich Golf Club
Estate Publications

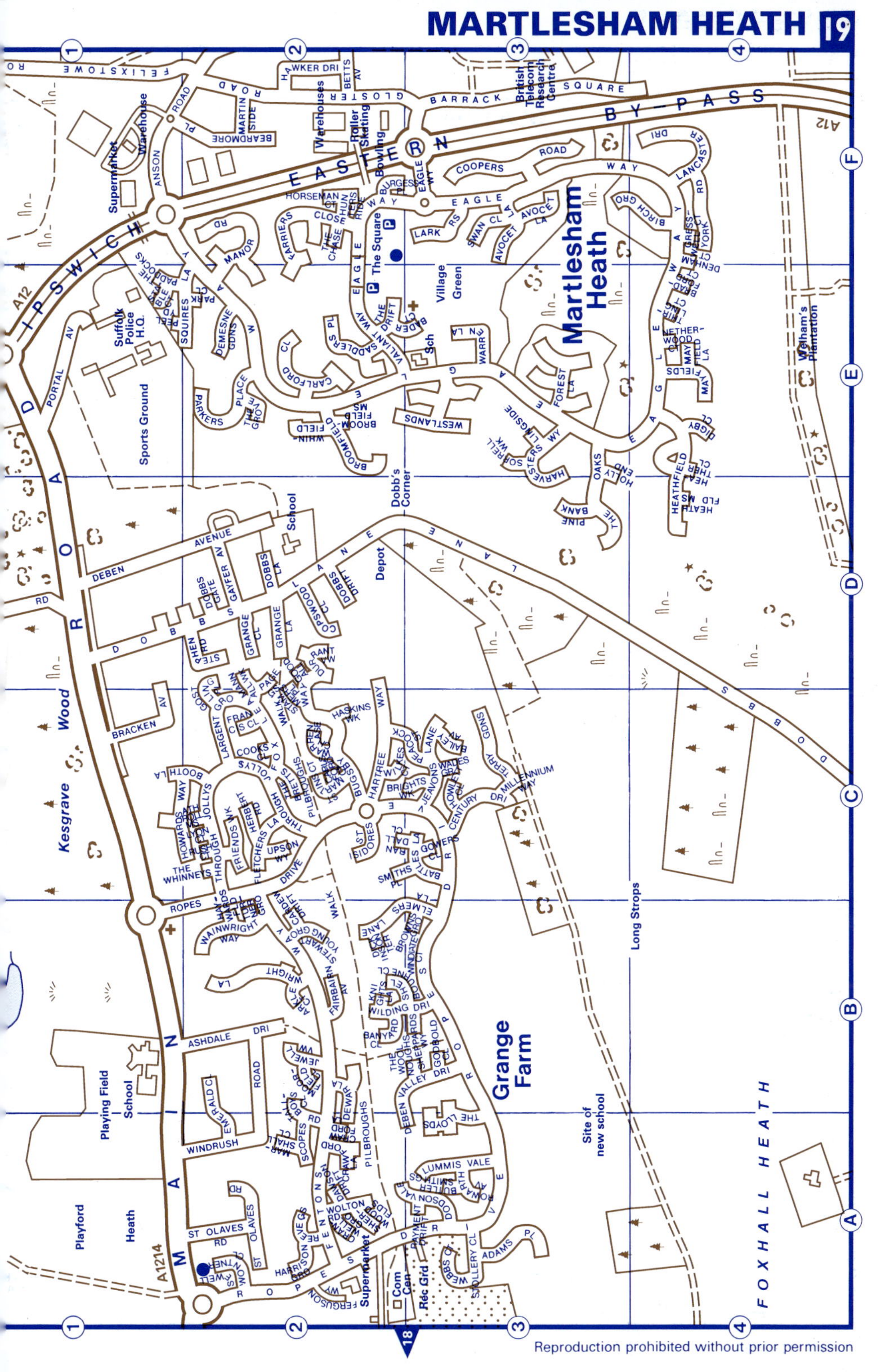

MARTLESHAM HEATH
Martlesham Heath
Grange Farm
IPSWICH ROAD
EASTERN BY-PASS
FELIXSTOWE RD
A12
FOXHALL HEATH
Kesgrave Wood
Playford Heath
Playing Field
Supermarket
Warehouse
Suffolk Police H.Q.
Sports Ground
School
Dobb's Corner
Depot
Village Green
British Telecom Research Centre
Welham's Plantation
Site of new school
Long Strops
Reproduction prohibited without prior permission
HAWKER DRI
BETTS AV
GLOSTER
BARRACK
SQUARE
ANSON RD
MARTIN PL
BEARDMORE
BADMORE SIDE
MANOR RD
SQUIRES LA
PARK PADDOCKS
THE PADDOCK
PORTAL AV
PELL AV
DEMESNE GDNS
PARKERS
THE PLACE
THE GROVE
FARRIERS
THE CHASE
CLOSE
HORSEMAN CT
BURGESS PIERS
HUNTERS
EAGLE WAY
SADDLERS PL
VALIANT WAY
BADER DRI
CARLFORD CL
WHIN FIELD
BROOM FIELD
BROOMFIELD MS
WESTLANDS
COOPERS ROAD
EAGLE
LARK RS
SWAN CLA
AVOCET LA
AVOCET CL
WARREN LA
WARRE
FOREST LA
HARVESTERS
SORRELL WK
LINGSIDE
OAKS
HOLLY END
THE BANK
PINE BANK
BIRCH GRO
LANCASTER DRI
DENHAM
CRESS CT
YORK CT
NETHERWOOD
MAYFIELD
MAYFIELDS
DIGBY CL
HEATHER
HEATHFIELD MS
FLD CL
HEATH FLD
A12
DEBEN
AVENUE
RD
DEBEN ROAD
BRACKEN AV
DOBBS GATE
DOBBS CL
GAYFER AV
GRANGE CL
GRANGE LA
STEPHEN RD
COPSWOOD CL
DOBBS DRIFT
LARGENT GROVE
LINGFIELD
GOSLING CL
FRANCIS CL
COOKS
JOLLYS
HOWARDS WAY
BOOTH LA
THE WHINNETS
THROUGH RD
LYON JOLLYS
FRIENDS WK
FLETCHERS LA
HERBERT RD
UPSON WAY
ROPES
WAINWRIGHT WAY
WARDS
NERO
STEWART WAY
YOUNG GRO
WALK
CADET WAY
ARKLE LA
WRIGHT
FAIRBAIRN AV
HASKINS WK
WILLES WAY
BAILEY WAY
PEACOCK
JEAVONS LA
GOWERS
CENTURY DRI
MILLENNIUM WAY
TERRY GDNS
HARTREE WAY
BRIGHTS
CHOWLE DRI
SMITHS PL
BATTLES LA
ELMERS LANE
BROWNS
WINTER
GIFTS
BANYARD CL
WILDING DRI
SHEPARDS DRI
WOOLNOUGHS
THE LLOYDS
GODBOLD DRI
DEBEN VALLEY
FENTONS
CRAWFORD RD
WOLTON RD
HARRISON GRO
FERGUSON
DEWAR LA
PILBROUGHS
MARSHALL CL
SCOPES
BOTT RD
BOSTOCK RD
WINDRUSH
ASHDALE DRI
EMERALD CL
JEWELL WAY
MEDLEY
ST OLAVES RD
MONTNER
WEBBS CL
SADLERY CL
ADAMS PL
LUMMIS VALE
BUTLER
DOTSON
SMITHS
ROMARTH AV
PAYMENT
DRIFT
Con Cen
Rec Grd
Supermarket
A1214

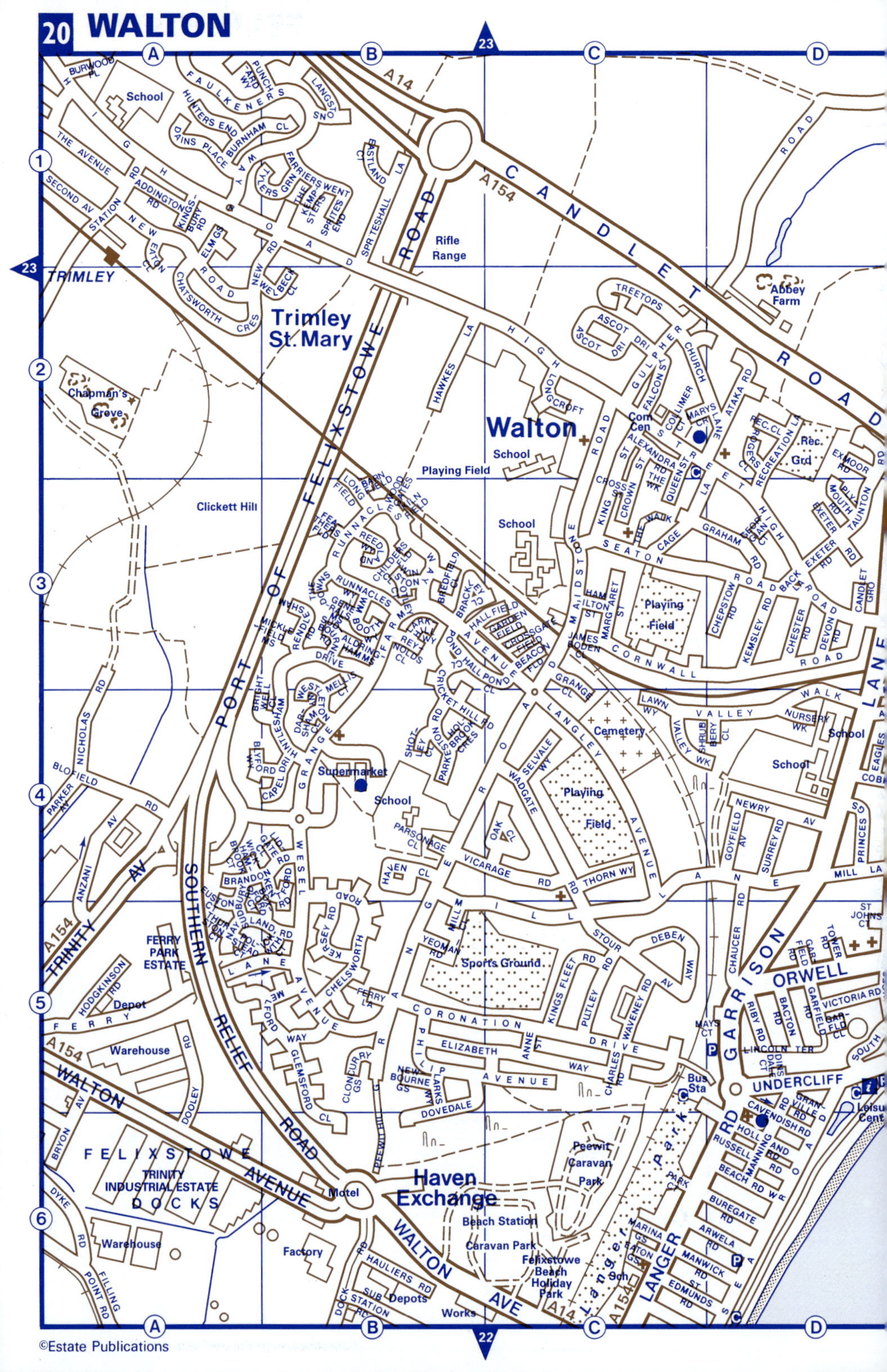

20 WALTON
23
A14
A154
CANDLET ROAD
TRIMLEY
BURWOOD PL
School
THE AVENUE
SECOND AV
FAULKENERS
HUNTERS END
BURNHAM
PUNCHARD WY
LANGSTON
FARRIERS WENT
KEMPSTERS
SPRITES END
EASTLAND
SPRITESHALL LA
STATION RD
NEW EATON
ADDINGTONS RD
KINGSBURY RD
ELM GR
CHATSWORTH
NEW BECK CL
CRES
Trimley St. Mary
Clickett Hill
Chapman's Grove
PORT OF FELIXSTOWE ROAD
Rifle Range
HAWKES LA
HIGH
LONGCROFT
LONG
Walton
School
Playing Field
School
BARN FIELD
LONG FIELD
WOODS
FEATHERS FIELD
RUNNACLES
REEDLAND
CHILDERS FIELD
CROSS COTE
GENE BOOTH
MS
AYLDRING
TOWNS
RENDLESHAM
DRIVE
BOUR
HAMMS
MICKLEFIELD NS
WESTLETON CL
BRIGHT WELL
DARSHAM
DRINTLESHAM
MELLIS CT
CAPEL
GRANGE
BLOFIELD
NICHOLAS RD
BLYFORD WY
PARKER AV
ANZANI
TRINITY AV
A154
SOUTHERN
RELIEF
ROAD
FERRY PARK ESTATE
HODGKINSON
Depot
FERRY
Warehouse
WALTON AV
BRYON
DYKE RD
FILLING POINT RD
FELIXSTOWE
TRINITY
DOCKS
Warehouse
GLEMSFORD
DOOLEY RD
BRANDON RD
EUSTON CT
TOLSTEAD
WORK HSE LA
LID GATE RD
WESEL RD
KERSEY RD
CHELSWORTH
FERRY LA
CLONCURRY GDNS
Motel
Factory
HAULIERS RD
DOCK
SUB STATION
Depots
Works
WALTON AVE
A14
HAVEN CL
PARSONAGE CL
VICARAGE RD
SHOTLEY RD
PARKESTON
HOLBROOK CRES
CRICKET HILL RD
POND HALL RD
BRACKLEY
HALL FIELD
GARDEN FIELD
CROSSGATE FIELD
BEACON FLD
JAMES BODEN
GRANGE CL
LANGLEY
OAK CL
WADGATE RD
SELVALE
NEW BOURNE RD
LARKS
DOVEDALE
PHILIP AVENUE
ELIZABETH
ANNE ST
CORONATION RD
YEOMAN RD
MILL
Sports Ground
KINGS FLEET RD
STOUR
WAVENEY RD
PLITLEY
DEBEN
THORN WY
Playing Field
Cemetery
LAWN WY
VALLEY WK
SHRUBBERY CL
VALLEY WK
NURSERY WK
School
School
WALK
EAGLES
COB
MILL LA
PRINCES RD
NEWRY AV
GOYFIELD AV
SURREY RD
CHAUCER
GARRISON
ORWELL
ST JOHNS CT
Com Cen
Walton School
TREETOPS
ASCOT DRI
ASCOT DRI
GULPHER RD
FALCONS ST
COLLIMER ST
CHURCH
MARYS CR
ATAKA RD
MAIDSTONE
KING
CROWN ST
CROSS ST
SEATON RD
HAM ILTON ST
MARGARET
ALEXANDRA RD
QUEENS
THE WK
CAGE
GRAHAM RD
THE WALK
CORNWALL
CHEPSTOW RD
KEMSLEY RD
CHESTER RD
DEVON RD
BACK RD
HIGH RD
REC CL
RECREATION LA
Rec. Grd
EXMOOR RD
PLYMOUTH
EXETER RD
TAUNTON RD
CANDLET GRO
Abbey Farm
VALLEY
MAYS CT
Bus Sta
GARRISON LA
RIBY RD
BACTON RD
DALE RD
LINCOLN TER
UNDERCLIFF
GRANVILLE RD
CAVENDISH RD
HOLL
MANNING RD
RUSSELL RD
BEACH RD
VICTORIA RD
GAR FLD
GARFIELD CL
TONER RD
SOUTH
Leisure Cent
BUREGATE RD
ARWELA RD
MANWICK RD
ST EDMUNDS RD
MARINA
EATON RD
Sch
LANGER ROAD
A154
A14
Peewit Caravan Park
Haven Exchange
Beach Station
Caravan Park
Felixstowe Beach Holiday Park
Supermarket
School
©Estate Publications
22

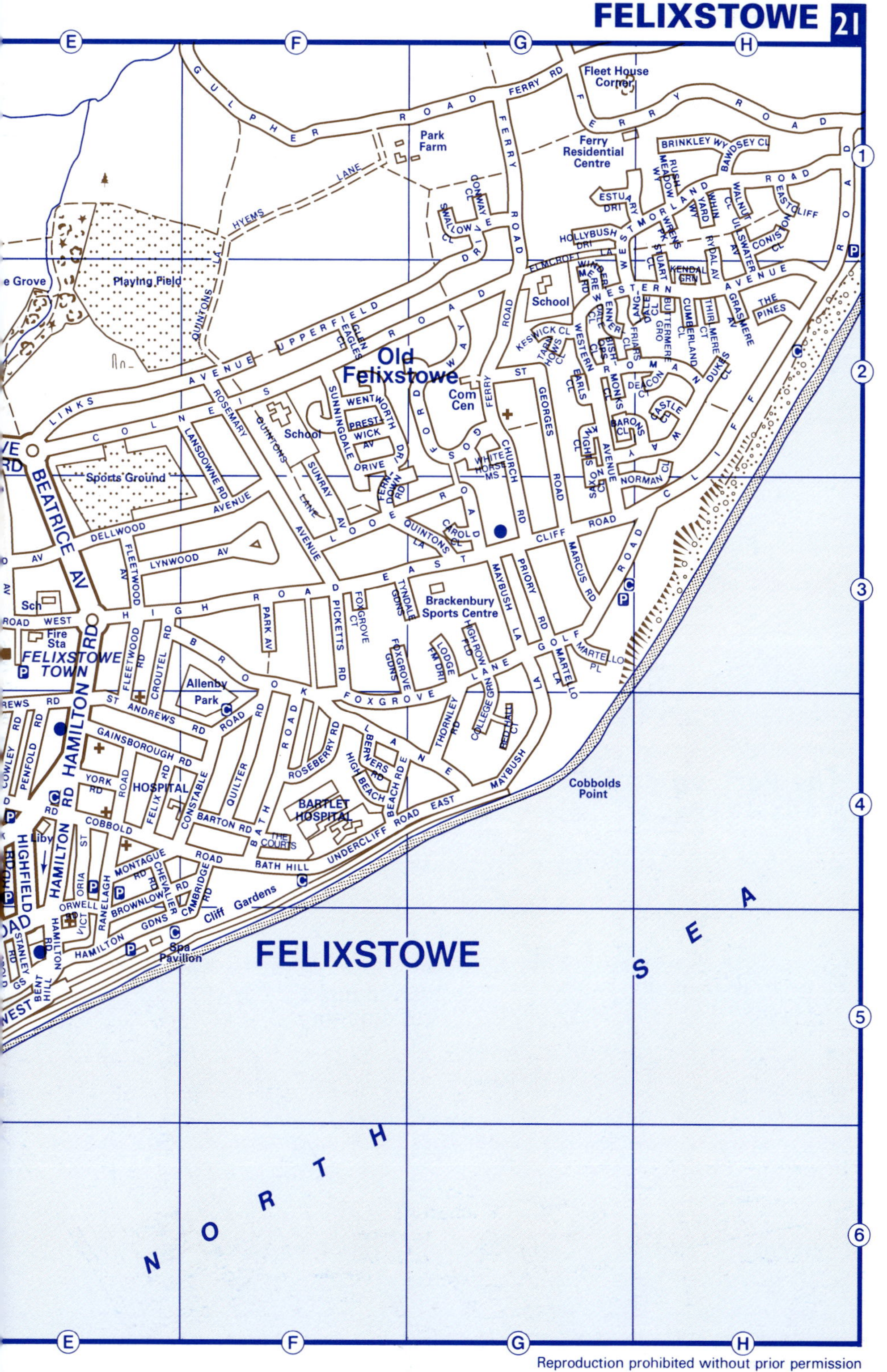
FELIXSTOWE
Fleet House Corner
Park Farm
Ferry Residential Centre
BRINKLEY WY
BAWDSEY CL
FERRY RD
FERRY ROAD
GULPHER ROAD
HYEMS LANE
DONWAY
SWALLOW CL
ESTUARY DRI
RUSHMEADOW WY
MORLAND PK
WRENS WY
WHIN YARD
WALNUT CL
RYDAL AV
EAST CLIFF
ROAD
CONISON CL
HOLLYBUSH DRI
WESTMOR
KENDAL GRN
Playing Field
e Grove
School
ELMCROFT LA
WINGER WINREN
WESTERN
STUART CT
ULSWATER AV
GRASMERE
THE PINES
THIRLMERE AV
CUMBERLAND AV
UPPERFIELD
GLEN EAGLES
Old Felixstowe
Com Cen
KESWICK CL
TARN CL
HOWS CL
EARLS CL
MONKS
BISH CL
FRIARS
DEACON
DUKES CL
LINKS
COLN
ROSEMARY
QUINTONS LA
AVENUE
School
WENTWORTH DRI
PREST WICK AV
SUNNINGDALE DRIVE
SUNRAY LANE
FERN DOWN RD
FORD ROAD
GEORGES ROAD
WHITE HORSE MS
CHURCH RD
BARONS CL
KNIGHTS CL
CASTLE CL
NORMAN
Sports Ground
LANSDOWNE RD
FLEETWOOD AV
DELLWOOD
LYNWOOD AV
SUNRAY AV
CAROL
QUINTONS LA
MAYBUSH LA
MARCUS RD
PRIORY RD
CLIFF ROAD
BEATRICE AV
Sch
ROAD WEST
Fire Sta
FELIXSTOWE TOWN
HIGH RD
CROUTEL RD
BROOK ROAD
PARK AV
PARK RD
PICKETTS RD
FOXGROVE CT
TYNDALE GDNS
FOXGROVE GDNS
Brackenbury Sports Centre
LODGE
FM DRI
HIGH RD
GOLF LA
MARTELLO PL
ANDREWS RD
Allenby Park
ST ANDREWS RD
CONSTABLE ROAD
QUILTER RD
BARTON RD
BATH RD
ROSEBERRY RD
FOXGROVE LANE
L BERNERS
HIGH BEACH
THORNLEY RD
BEACH RD E
COLLEGE GRN
RED CHALK CT
MAYBUSH
Cobbolds Point
PENFOLD RD
COWLEY RD
HAMILTON RD
GAINSBOROUGH RD
YORK RD
HOSPITAL
COBBOLD
FELIX RD
MONTAGUE RD
CHEVALIER RD
CAMBRIDGE RD
BARTLET HOSPITAL
THE COURTS
BATH HILL
UNDERCLIFF ROAD EAST
HIGHFIELD RD
ORWELL RD
VICTORIA RD
RANELAGH RD
BROWNLOW RD
GDNS
HAMILTON RD
STANLEY RD
BENT HILL
WEST
Cliff Gardens
Spa Pavilion
FELIXSTOWE
SEA
NORTH
Reproduction prohibited without prior permission

THE PORT OF FELIXSTOWE
FELIXSTOWE
The Port of Felixstowe
Harwich
Harbour
NORTH SEA
DOCKS
FELIXSTOWE
Landguard Common
Warehouse
Warehouses
Warehouse
TRINITY AVENUE
ANZANI AV
PARKER ROAD
FAGBURY ROAD
TRINITY ROAD
HODGKINSON RD
FERRY
Depot
WALTON
Depot
Depot
BRYON AV
BRYON AV
DYKE ROAD
NORTHERN SPINE ROAD
FILLING POINT ROAD
Trinity Terminal
Container Park
TRINITY INDUSTRIAL ESTATE
Warehouse
DOOLEY RD
GLEMSFORD CL
FERRY PARK ESTATE
SOUTHERN RELIEF ROAD
A14
LIDGATE WK
WOCK...
BRANDON
EUSTON
THURLOW
NAYLAND
NAUGHBURY
ROLFE CT
MELFORD
STEAD
LANE
WESEL AVENUE
CHELSWORTH AVENUE
WAY
BENTLEY
BRYON
HAM CT
KESGRAVE
NEWBOURNE
KERSEY RD
PHILIP
AVENUE
RANGE
CORONATION
DOVEDALE
ELIZABETH
LARKS
CL
ANNE
PHILIP GS
BOURNE GS
AVENUE
WAY
DRIVE
CHARLES RD
ANDREW CL
School
PARSONAGE CL
HAVEN CL
VICARAGE RD
OAK CL
WADGATE RD
THORN WY
MILL RD
KINGS FLEET RD
PUTLEY RD
STOUR RD
DEBEN WAY
WAVENEY RD
LANGLEY AV
Playing Field
YEOMAN RD
Sports Ground
MAYS CT
P
Bus Sta
Peewit Caravan Park
LANGER PARK ROAD
MARINA GS
EATON GS
SON
ARWEL
MANWICK
ST EDMUNDS RD
PLATTERS RD
MICKLEGATE RD
BEACH STA RD
LEVINGTON RD
TACONET RD
PRETTYMAN RD
ORFORD RD
A154
Haven Exchange
Beach Station
Caravan Park
Felixstowe Beach Holiday Park
HAULIERS RD
Factory
Motel
WALTON AVENUE
SUB-STATION
Depots
Works
Sewage Works
Factory
DOCK RD
STONE RD
Tank Farm
Depot
Warehouses
Container Park
Factory
Amb Sta
Com Cen
Coastguard Station
Martello Tower
Ship Ferry Terminal (Vehicular)
Transit Shed
Container Park
Warehouse
Container Park
Mills
COLD STORE ROAD
GROVE RD
Dock Basin
Warehouse
Warehouse
Transit Shed
Fire Sta.
Ship Ferry Terminal (Vehicular)
DOCK ROAD
SUNDERLAND RD
DARRELL RD
ADASTRAL CL
ADASTRAL CLOSE
CARR ROAD
Suffolk Sands Holiday Park
TERRACE
MANOR RD
Custom House
Transit Shed
LANDGUARD
POINT VIEW WAY
Landguard Common
Landguard Terminal
MANOR RD
Landguard Caravan Park
P
Depot
Landguard Fort (casemated)
Belfast Jetty
OYSTER BED RD
FERRY LA
WAY
20

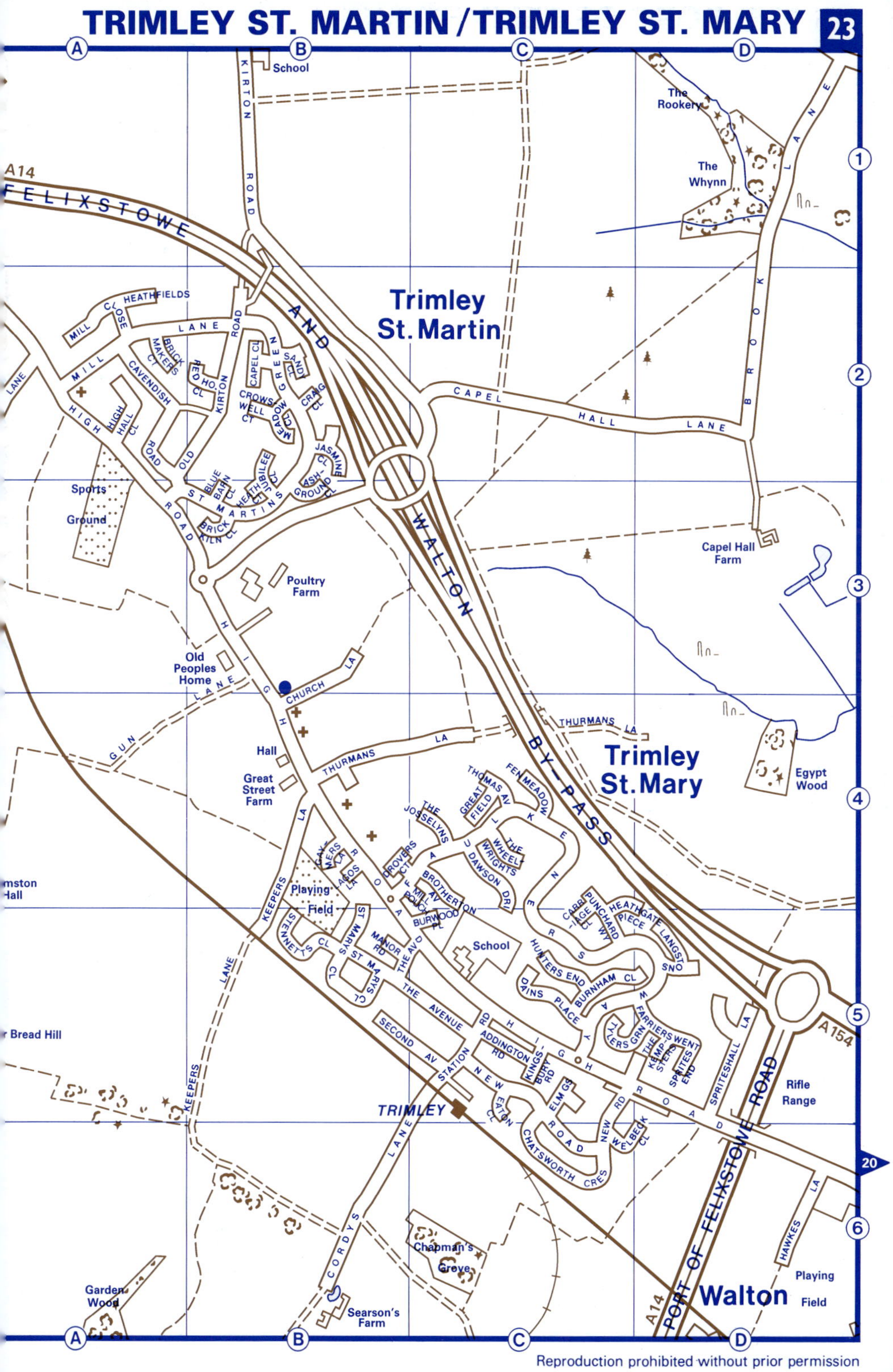

A B C D
1 2 3 4 5 6
20
A14
FELIXSTOWE
The Rookery
The Whynn
School
KIRTON ROAD
Trimley St.Martin
HEATHFIELDS
MILL CLOSE
MILL LANE
BRICK MAKERS CT
CAVENDISH
RED HO. CL
KIRTON CL
HIGH HALL CL
HIGH HALL
OLD ROAD
ST. MARTINS ROAD
BRICK KILN CL
BLUE BARN
CAPEL CL
CROWS WELL CT
MEADOW GREEN
SAND CL
CRAIG CL
JASMINE CL
JUBILEE CL
HEATHFIELD CT
ASH-GROUND CL
WALTON
CAPEL HALL LANE
Sports Ground
Poultry Farm
Old Peoples Home
Great Street Farm
Hall
CHURCH LA
HIGH LANE
GUN LANE
THURMANS LA
BY-PASS
THURMANS LA
Capel Hall Farm
Egypt Wood
Trimley St.Mary
KEEPERS LANE
Playing Field
THE JOSSELYNS
GREAT FIELD
THOMAS AV
FEN MEADOW
KEEPERS
DROVERS CT
BROTHERTON AV
MILL CL
BURWOOD PL
DAWSON DRI
THE WHEEL WRIGHTS
LAGOS LA
STENNET'S CL
ST MARYS CL
MANOR RD
ST MARYS RD
THE AV
School
Hunters End
DAINS PLACE
CABBAGE CL
PUNCHARD WY
BURNHAM CL
HEATHGATE
LANGSTON PIECE
FARRIERS GRN
KEMP STEPS
SPRITES END
FARRIERS WENT
SPRITESHALL LA
THE AVENUE
SECOND AV
STATION LANE
ADDINGTON RD
KINGS-BUR-RD
NEW EATON RD
ELMGS CL
HIGH ROAD
NEW RD
WELBECK CL
CHATSWORTH CRES
PORT OF FELIXSTOWE ROAD
A154
Rifle Range
TRIMLEY
CORDYS LANE
Chapman's Grove
Searson's Farm
Garden Wood
Bread Hill
lmston Hall
HAWKES LA
A14
Walton
Playing Field

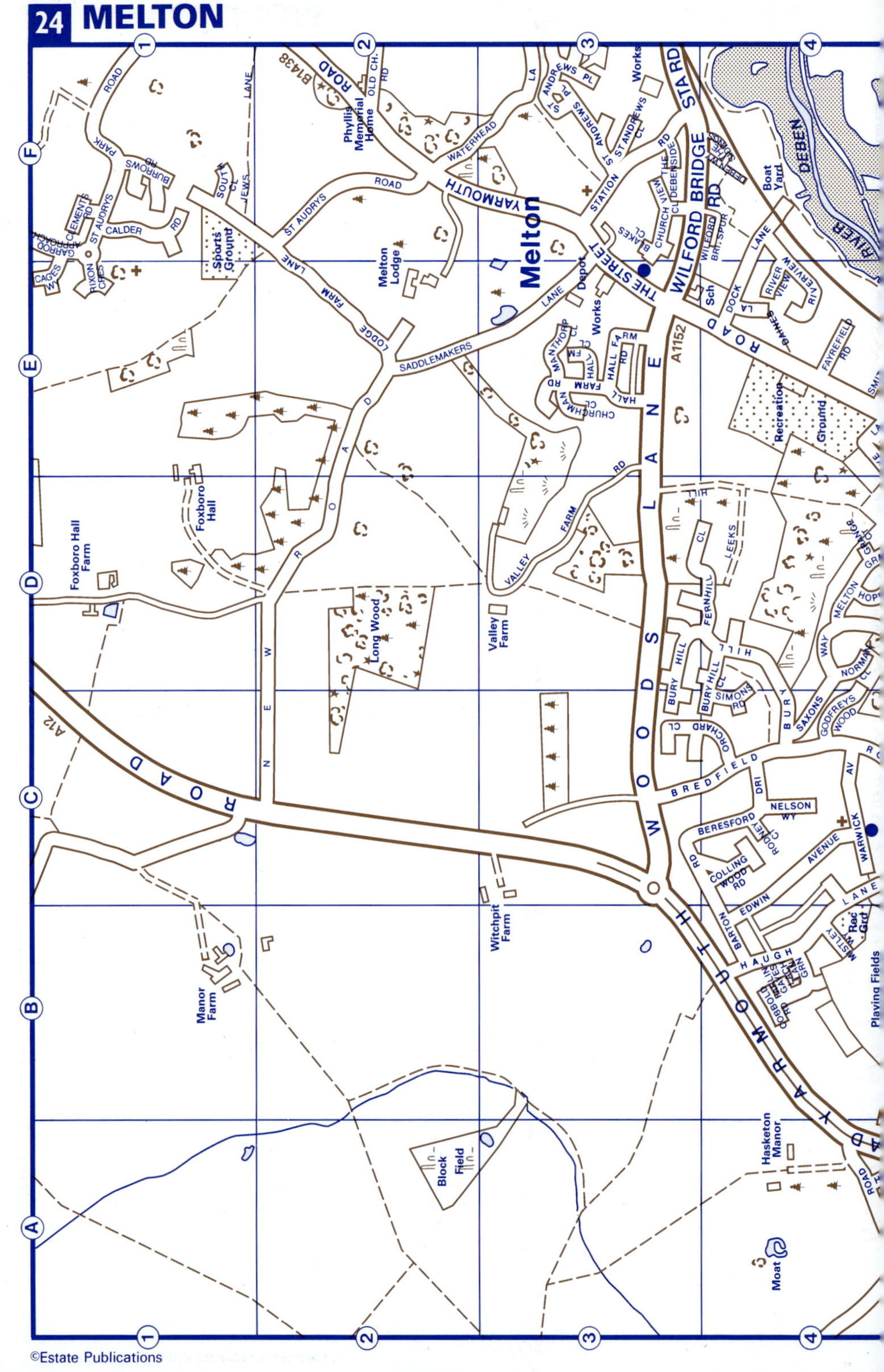
24 MELTON
DEBEN
RIVER
B1438
ROAD
OLD CH.
OLD RD
Phyllis Memorial Home
WATERHEAD
ST ANDREWS PL
LA
ST ANDREWS PL
ST ANDREWS RD
Works
STATION RD
THE STREET
STA RD
WILFORD BRIDGE
CHURCH VIEW CL
DEBENSIDE
WILFORD RD
BAKES CL
Boat Yard
RIVER VIEW
BARNES LA
DOCK LA
Sch
YARMOUTH
ROAD
SOUTH CL
JEWS LANE
ST AUDRYS
ST AUDRYS LANE
BURROWS RD
PARK RD
CLEMENTS RD
GARROD APPROACH
ST AUDRYS RD
CALDER RD
RIXON CRES
CAGES WAY
Sports Ground
Melton
Melton Lodge
LODGE FARM LANE
SADDLEMAKERS
A1152
ROAD
FAYREFIELD RD
Recreation Ground
LANE
Depot
Works
MANTHORP CL
CHURCHMAN RD
HALL FARM
HALL FARM RD
HALL FARM CL
Foxboro Hall
Foxboro Hall Farm
NEW ROAD
Long Wood
Valley Farm
VALLEY FARM RD
HILL
LEEKS
FERNHILL CL
BURY HILL
BURY HILL CL
SIMONS RD
HILL
MELTON HOP GR
WAY
GR
NORMAN CL
SAXONS
GODFREYS WOOD
BURY
ORCHARD CL
WOODS LANE
BREDFIELD
A12
ROAD
Manor Farm
Witchpit Farm
Block Field
Hasketon Manor
Moat
YARMOUTH ROAD
BERESFORD
COLLING WOOD RD
RONEY RD
DRI
NELSON WY
WARWICK AVENUE
AVENUE
AV
RD
Rec Grd
Playing Fields
MISTLEY LANE
EDWIN
BARTON RD
HAUGH
COBBOLD RD
GATACRE GRN
FP
GAINSBOROUGH GRN
Rec Grd

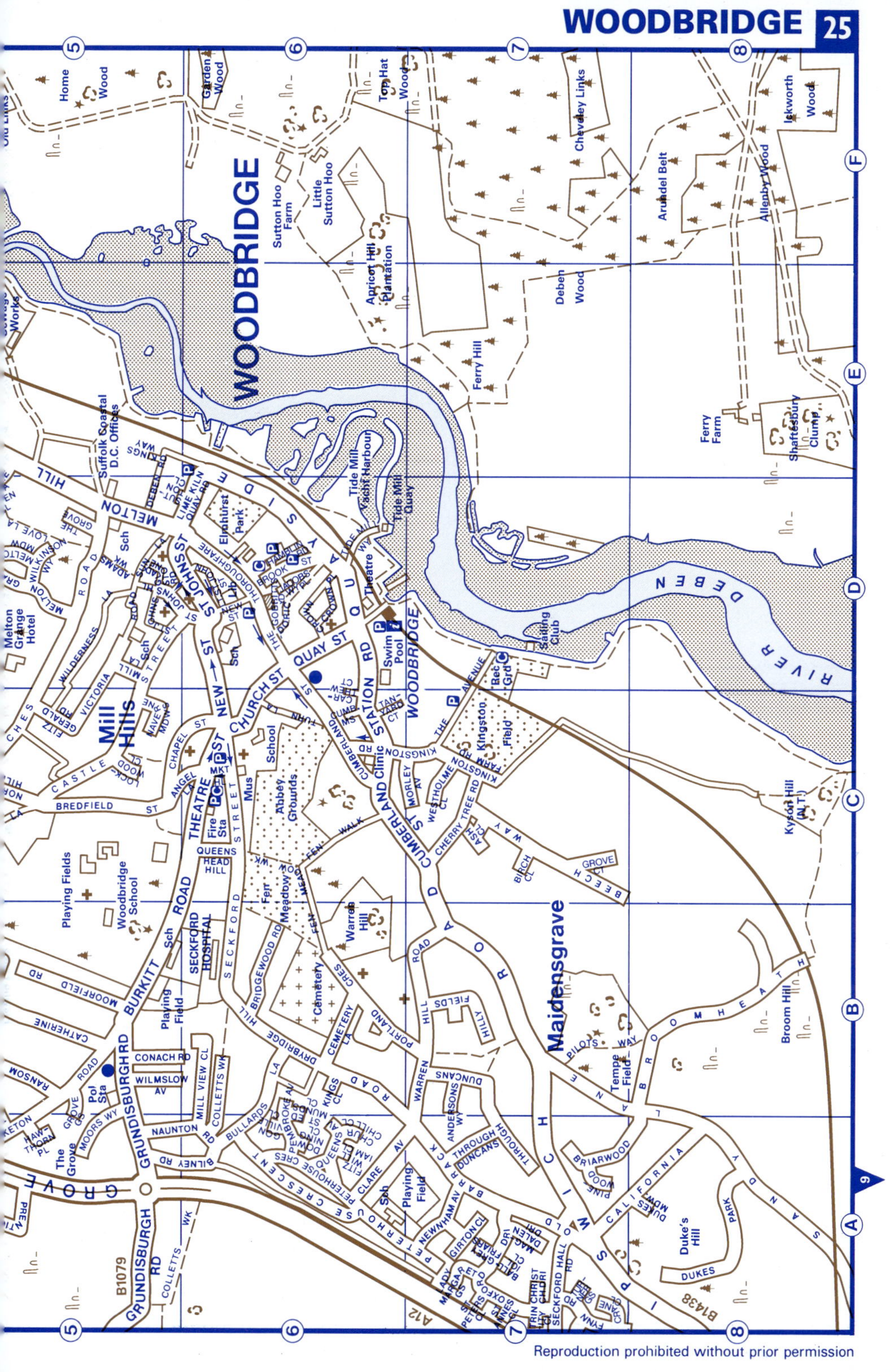
WOODBRIDGE
Home
Wood
Garden Wood
Chevaley Links
Ickworth Wood
Sutton Hoo Farm
Little Sutton Hoo
Top Hat Wood
Arundel Belt
Allenby Wood
Apricot Hill Plantation
Deben Wood
Ferry Hill
Ferry Hill
Ferry Farm
Shaftesbury Clump
Works
MELTON HILL
Suffolk Coastal D.C. Offices
KINGS WAY
DEBEN CT
LIME KILN QUAY RD
Elmhurst Park
Tide Mill
Yacht Harbour
Tide Mill Quay
RIVER DEBEN
Sailing Club
Melton Grange Hotel
MELTON METH
WILKINSON
MDW
LOVE LA
THE GROVE
ADAMS WK
ST JOHNS ST
ST JOHNS
STHORN
THOROUGHFARE
BROOK ST
FRANKLIN RD
JOBS YD
NEW ST
CROWN PL
THE GOBBINS
Theatre
Swim Pool
QUAY ST
QUAY ST
STATION RD
WOODBRIDGE
STATION
Swim Pool
THE AVENUE
Bec Grd
Kingston Field
Mill Hills
FITZ GERALD RD
VICTORIA
MILL
LOCK WOOD
MAVER MDWG
Chapel St
Angel La
THEATRE ST
Fire Sta
POL STA
MKT
Church St
NEW ST
MUS
School
Abbey Grounds
CUMBERLAND RD
CUMBERLAND Clinic
CAR TAN YARD CT
KINGSTON
MORLEY AV
WESTHOLME CL
KINGSTON FARM RD
Kingston Field
CHES
CASTLE ST
WILDERNESS
BREDFIELD ST
Playing Fields
Woodbridge School
SECKFORD HOSPITAL
BURKITT
MOORFIELD RD
Sch
Playing Field
SECKFORD ST
Queens Head Hill
Mus
Ferr WK
FEN MEADOW RD
FEN WK
Cemetery
Warren Hill
CEMETERY LA
CRES
PORTLAND FIELDS
HILLY
ASH CL
CHERRY TREE RD
BIRCH CL
BEECH
GROVE
Maidensgrave
BROOM HEATH
Broom Hill
Kyson Hill (NT)
RANSOM
HAWS THORN PL
The Grove
MOORS WY
GROVE
Pol Sta
CATHERINE
GRUNDISBURGH RD
CONACH RD
WILMSLOW AV
NAUNTON RD
BILNEY RD
BULLARDS
MILL VIEW CL
COLLETTS WK
PEMBROKE AV
DOWNING CT
MUNDS CL
QUEENS CL
KINGS CL
ROAD
WARREN HILL
DUNCANS
ANDERSONS WY
THROUGH DUNCANS
BARRACK
PILOTS WAY
Tempe Field
PINE WOOD
BRIARWOOD
CALIFORNIA
DUKES MDW
Duke's Hill
DUKES
PARK
B1438
B1079
GRUNDISBURGH RD
COLLETTS WK
PRESTON
KELTON
GROVE
RANSOM
PREM
PETERHOUSE CRESCENT
CLARE AV
NEWNHAM AV
FITZ WM CT
CHILL CT
Sch
Playing Field
LADY MARGARET CT
GIRTON CL
OXFORD RD
BALLIOL CL
DALEH DRI
FRIARS CL
PETERS RD
ST ANNES CL
TRIN CHRIST CLY CHDRI
Seckford Hall
FYNN
CRANE LA
NANS CL
CHURCH
WOLD
CALIFORNIA
SANDY
A12
Reproduction prohibited without prior permission

CLAYDON

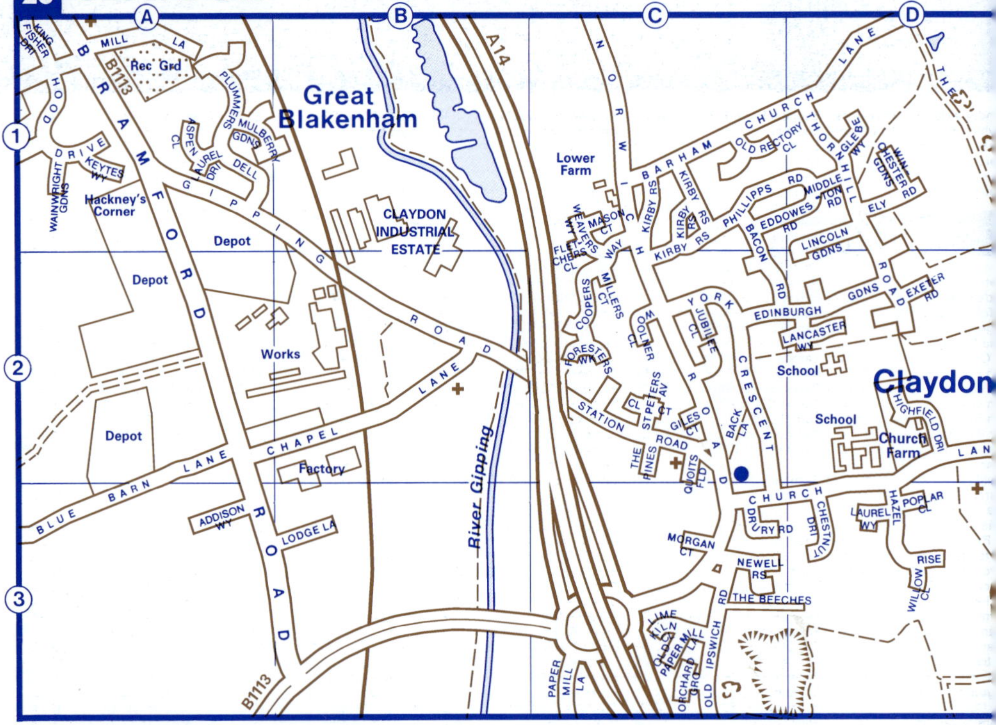

Great Blakenham

Lower Farm

CLAYDON INDUSTRIAL ESTATE

Claydon

Rec Grd

Hackney's Corner

Depot

Depot

Depot

Works

Factory

Station

School

School

Church Farm

River Gipping

KING FISHER DRI
WAINWRIGHT GDNS
BRAMFORD ROAD
B1113
MILL LA
KEYTES WY
ASPEN CL
LAUREL DRI
MULBERRY DELL
PLUMMERS GDNS
GIPPING ROAD
BLUE BARN LANE
CHAPEL LANE
ADDISON WY
LODGE LA
B1113

BARHAM
CHURCH LANE
OLD RECTORY CL
KIRBY RS
KIRBY RS
KIRBY RS
KIRBY RS
THORNHILL
GLEBE WY
CHESTER RD
WINN RD
ELY GDNS
PHILLIPPS RD
EDDOWES RD
BACON RD
MIDDLETON RD
LINCOLN GDNS
EXETER RD
GDNS
ROAD
WEAVERS CL
FLETCHERS CL
MASON WAY
ST WAY
MILLERS CL
WOOLNER CL
EDINBURGH
LANCASTER WY
COOPERS CL
FORESTERS WK
YORK CL
JUBILEE CL
BACK LA
CRESCENT
HIGHFIELD DRI
THE PINES
ST PETERS AV
GILES CT
QUOITS FLD
DRURY RD
CHURCH LANE
CHESTNUT DRI
LAUREL WY
HAZEL CL
POPLAR CL
MORGAN CT
NEWELL RS
THE BEECHES
WILLOW CL
RISE
LIME KILN
OLD PAPER MILL
ORCHARD LA
OLD IPSWICH RD
PAPER MILL LA
NORWICH
A14

CAPEL ST. MARY

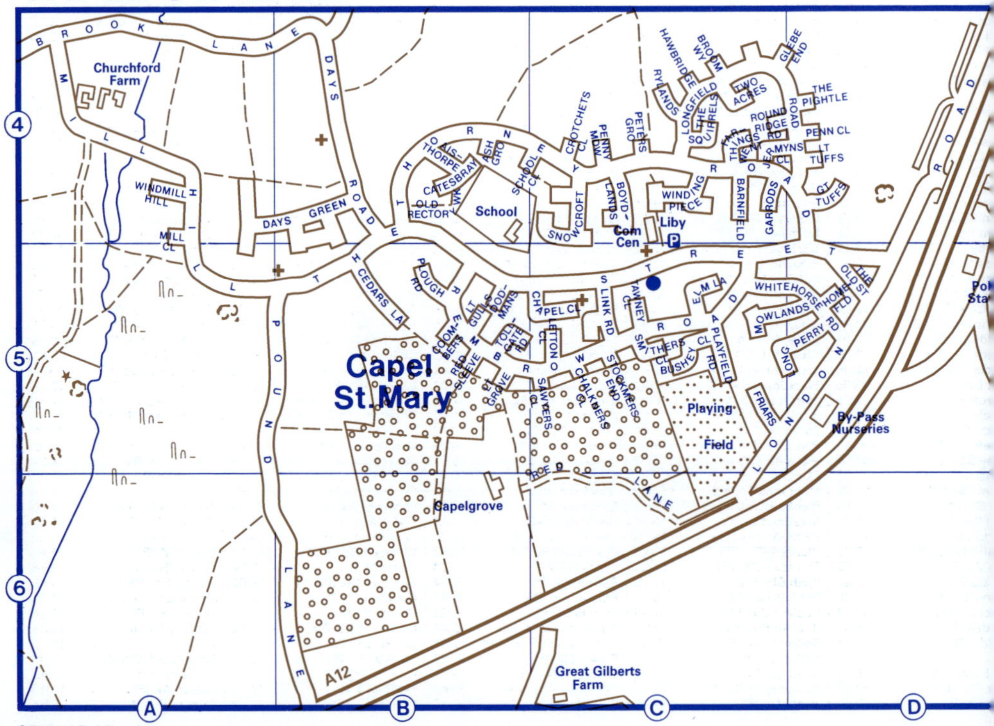

Churchford Farm

Capel St. Mary

School

Liby

Com Cen

Playing Field

Capelgrove

Great Gilberts Farm

By-Pass Nurseries

BROOK LANE
MILL
DAYS ROAD
WINDMILL HILL
MILL CL
DAYS GREEN
CEDARS LA
PLOUGH RD
POUND LANE
THORPE
CATESBRAY
OLD RECTORY
ASH GRO
SCHOOL CL
CROTCHETS
SNOWCROFT
BOYD'S LANDS
CHAPEL CT
PLOUGH RD
COOMBERS
SLEEVE CL
GUTHRUMS GRO
TOLLGATE RD
LETTON RD
SAWYERS
CHALKNERS CL
LINK RD
SMITHERS
AWNEY
STOCKMERS END
ELM LA
BUSHEY CL
STREET
RYLANDS
HAWBRIDGE WY
LONGFIELD
BROOM WY
THE SQUIRRELS
PENNY MDW
PETERS GRO
TWO ACRES
GLEBE END
ROUND RIDGE
THANGS RD
KINGS VIEW
THE PIGHTLE
PENN CL
ROAD
LT TUFFS
GT TUFFS
MYNS CL
JEFFRIES CL
WINDING PIECE
BARNFIELD
GARRODS
WHITEHORSE LANE
ROWLANDS
HOMEFLD
OLD ST
PERRY RD
PLAYFIELD
LONG ROAD
FRIARS
THE
Po Sta
A12

...ndex includes some names
...which there is insufficient
... on the maps. These names
...receded by an * and are
...ved by the nearest adjoining
...ughfare.

IPSWICH

Street	Ref
...tsbury Clo. IP2	15 F2
...deen Way. IP4	9 E6
...foyle Clo. IP4	9 F5
...gdon Clo. IP2	15 E2
...ia Clo. IP3	17 G2
... Gro. IP8	14 B2
...n Clo. IP2	14 B1
...n Clo. IP8	6 A4
...n Gdns. IP8	6 A4
...n Rd. IP8	6 A4
... Rd. IP1	11 E1
...ns Clo. IP2	12 B6
...ns Pl. IP5	19 A3
...aide Rd. IP4	13 H3
...iral Rd. IP8	14 D3
...e Clo. IP1	6 D6
...ie Rd. IP1	11 H3
... Rd. IP3	13 E5
...ta Clo. IP5	18 D1
...croft Clo. IP1	7 G4
...croft Rd. IP1	7 G4
...lee. IP2	15 E3
...man Rd. IP1	5 A2
...andra Rd. IP4	5 F1
...aints Rd. IP1	11 G1
...by Rd. IP2	11 F3
...llows Ct. IP3	16 C2
...gton Clo. IP4	13 E2
... Clo. IP4	8 D6
...ndhayes. IP2	11 H6
... St. IP1	11 H2
...n Rd. IP3	13 E5
...ster Rd. IP2	11 H5
...os Clo. IP3	16 D3
...l La. IP4	5 D3
...l Rd. IP8	6 A5
...esea Rd. IP1	11 H2
...a Parkway Nth.	6 D2
...a Parkway Sth.	6 C3
...s Clo. IP4	9 E5
... Clo East. IP2	11 F3
... Clo West. IP2	11 F3
...St. IP1	11 H2
...rook Rd. IP2	14 D2
...n Rd. IP5	19 F1
...m Rd. IP1	6 D5
...eby Clo. IP2	14 C2
...de St. IP1	5 B2
...angel Clo. IP2	11 F4
...e St. IP4	5 E2
... Ct. IP5	19 B2
...right Rd. IP2	11 F2
...d Clo. IP1	7 F4
...rs Ter. IP4	5 E2
...del Way. IP3	13 H5
...t Dri. IP3	13 F5
...roft Rd. IP1	7 F5
...ale Dri. IP5	19 B2
...own Way. IP3	13 H6
...eld Ct. IP4	13 E4
...y St. IP2	12 B5
...here Gro. IP4	12 D3
...on Clo. IP2	14 C1
... Rd. IP2	11 F5
...n Clo. IP1	6 C5
...ton Rd. IP2	14 D2
...ll Mews. IP5	19 C2
... Ct. IP1	5 C2
...sta Clo. IP3	17 G4
...n St. IP2	12 B5
...et La. IP5	19 F3
...dale Rd. IP3	16 D1
...d. IP4	9 F5
... Hamlet. IP3	5 F4
...r Clo. IP3	17 F1
...r Ct. IP5	19 E3

Street	Ref
Badgers Bank. IP2	14 D2
Badshah Av. IP3	13 F6
Bailey Av. IP5	19 C3
Bailey Clo. IP2	11 F3
Baird Clo. IP2	11 F2
Bakey Av. IP5	19 C3
Baldry Clo. IP8	14 B2
Ballater Clo. IP1	7 E3
Balmoral Clo. IP2	15 E2
Bank Rd. IP4	5 F1
Bantoft Ter. IP3	13 G6
Banyard Clo. IP5	19 B2
Barker Clo. IP2	10 D3
Barnham Pl. IP5	18 B3
Baronsdale Clo. IP1	7 G5
Barrack Corner. IP1	5 A1
Barrack La. IP1	5 A1
Barrack Sq. IP5	19 F3
Bartholomew St. IP4	12 D3
Barton Clo. IP2	14 D2
Bath St. IP2	12 B5
Battles La. IP5	19 C3
Beaconsfield Rd. IP1	11 G2
Beardmore Pl. IP5	19 F2
Beatrice Clo. IP3	13 E6
Beatty Rd. IP3	17 E1
Beaufort St. IP1	11 H2
Bedford St. IP1	5 B1
Beech Clo. IP8	10 B2
Beech Gro, Ipswich. IP3	13 E5
Beech Gro, Rushmere St Andrew. IP5	18 B2
Beech Rd. IP5	18 B2
Beechcroft Rd. IP1	7 F5
Bell Clo. IP2	12 B5
Bell La. IP5	18 D1
Belle Vue Rd. IP4	12 D3
Belmont Rd. IP2	14 B1
Belstead Av. IP2	12 A5
Belstead Rd. IP2	11 G6
Belvedere Rd. IP4	12 C1
Benacre Rd. IP3	16 D1
Benezet St. IP1	11 H2
Bennett Rd. IP1	6 D6
Bent La. IP4	18 B1
Bentley La. IP8	14 A6
Bentley Rd. IP1	6 C5
Berkeley Clo. IP4	8 C6
Bermuda Rd. IP3	17 G4
Bernard Cres. IP3	16 D1
Berners St. IP1	5 A1
Berry Clo. IP3	17 H2
Betts Av. IP5	19 F2
Beverley Rd. IP4	12 D1
Bibb Way. IP1	11 H3
Bildeston Gdns. IP4	8 B6
Birch Gro. IP5	19 F4
Birchcroft Rd. IP1	7 G4
Birchwood Dri. IP5	9 H5
Birkfield Clo. IP2	11 G5
Birkfield Dri. IP2	11 F6
Bishops Hill. IP3	12 D5
Bittern Clo. IP2	11 F5
Bixley Dri. IP4	18 B4
Bixley La. IP4	18 B4
Bixley Rd. IP3	13 G6
Black Horse La. IP1	5 B2
Blackdown Av. IP5	18 B2
Blackfriars Ct. IP4	5 D3
Blackthorn Clo. IP3	17 H2
Bladen Dri. IP4	18 B4
Blair Clo. IP4	18 B4
Blake Rd. IP1	7 F3
Blanche St. IP4	5 E2
Blandford Rd. IP3	13 H6
Blenheim Rd. IP1	11 G1
Blickling Clo. IP2	15 F1
Bloomfield St. IP4	13 F3
Bluebell Clo. IP2	11 F5
Bluestem Rd. IP3	17 G3
Blyth Clo. IP2	15 F2
Bobbits La. IP2	15 E3
Bodiam Clo. IP3	18 A5
Bodiam Rd. IP3	13 H5
Bodmin Clo. IP5	18 C3
Bolton La. IP4	5 D1
Bond St. IP4	5 D3
Bonnington Rd. IP3	16 C2
Booth La. IP5	19 C2

Street	Ref
Borrowdale Av. IP4	8 B6
Boss Hall Rd. IP1	11 E2
Bostock Rd. IP2	15 G2
Boston Rd. IP4	13 E2
Bourne Hill. IP2	15 G4
Bowland Dri. IP8	14 B2
Bowthorpe Clo. IP1	11 H2
Boyton Rd. IP3	16 D3
Bracken Av. IP5	19 C1
Brackenbury Clo. IP1	11 H1
Brackenhayes Clo. IP2	11 H6
Bradford Ct. IP5	19 E4
Bradley St. IP2	12 B5
Bramble Dri. IP3	17 H2
Bramblewood. IP8	14 B1
Bramford La. IP1	6 D5
Bramford Rd. IP1	11 E1
Bramhall Clo. IP2	14 C2
Bramley Chase. IP4	13 F2
Bransby Gdns. IP4	12 C2
Braziers Wood Rd. IP3	16 D3
Brecon Clo. IP2	15 G1
Brendon Dri. IP5	18 B3
Brettenham Cres. IP4	8 A6
Briarhayes Clo. IP2	11 H6
Brickfield Clo. IP2	12 B5
Bridge St. IP1	5 C4
Bridgwater Rd. IP2	14 C1
Bridle Way. IP1	12 B1
Bridport Av. IP3	13 H5
Brights Wk. IP5	19 C3
Brimstone Rd. IP8	14 D3
Brisbane Rd. IP4	13 H3
Bristol Rd. IP4	13 E2
Britannia Rd. IP4	13 F2
Broad Meadow. IP8	14 B1
Broadlands Way. IP4	18 B4
Broadmere Rd. IP1	11 F1
Broadway La. IP1	7 E5
Brockley Cres. IP1	6 D6
Broke Av. IP8	6 B4
Broke Hall Gdns. IP3	13 H5
Bromeswell Rd. IP4	8 B5
Bromley Clo. IP2	12 B6
Brook View. IP2	14 D2
Brookfield Rd. IP1	7 F6
Brookhill Way. IP4	18 B5
Brooks Hall Rd. IP1	11 G1
Broom Cres. IP3	16 C2
Broom Hill Rd. IP1	11 G1
Broomfield. IP5	19 E2
Broomfield Common. IP8	10 C3
Broomfield Mews. IP5	19 E2
Broomhayes. IP2	15 F1
Broughton Rd. IP1	11 H1
Browning Rd. IP1	7 E3
Browns Gro. IP5	19 B3
Brownsea Ct. IP5	19 C3
Brunel Rd. IP2	11 F3
Brunswick Rd. IP4	12 D1
Buckfast Clo. IP2	15 F1
Bucklesham Rd. IP3	13 H6
Bucks Horns La. IP8	14 A5
Buddleia Clo. IP2	11 F5
Bude Clo. IP5	18 C3
Bugsby Way. IP5	19 C2
Bullen Clo. IP8	6 A5
Bullen La. IP8	6 A5
Bulstrode Rd. IP2	12 B5
Bulwer Rd. IP1	11 H2
Bunting Rd. IP2	11 E6
Bunyan Clo. IP1	7 F4
Burgess Pl. IP5	19 F2
Burghley Clo. IP2	15 F1
Burke Clo. IP2	7 F4
Burke Rd. IP1	7 F4
Burlington Rd. IP1	5 A1
Burnet Clo. IP8	14 D3
Burnham Clo. IP4	13 E2
Burns Rd. IP1	7 E4
Burrell Rd. IP2	5 B4
Burstall La. IP8	10 A3
Bury Rd. IP1	6 C3
Bushman Gdns. IP8	6 A5
Butler Smith Gdns. IP5	19 A3
Butley Clo. IP2	15 E3
Butter Market. IP1	5 C2
Buttercup Clo. IP2	14 B2
Butterfly Gdns. IP4	18 B3

Street	Ref
Byland Clo. IP2	15 F1
Byron Rd. IP1	7 E3
Caithness Clo. IP4	9 E6
Camberley Rd. IP4	13 H2
Camborne Rd. IP5	18 D2
Cambridge Dri. IP2	14 D2
Cambridge Rd. IP5	18 C1
Camden Rd. IP3	13 F5
Campbell Rd. IP3	17 E2
Campion Rd. IP2	11 G5
Canberra Clo. IP4	13 H3
Canham St. IP1	5 A2
Canterbury Clo. IP2	15 E3
Canwood Gdns. IP3	13 F5
Cardew Drift. IP5	19 B2
Cardiff Av. IP2	15 G2
Cardigan St. IP1	11 H2
Carlford Clo. IP5	19 E2
Carlsford Ct. IP5	19 C2
Carlton Rd. IP5	18 C1
Carlton Way. IP4	8 C6
Carlyle Clo. IP1	7 F3
Carmarthen Clo. IP2	15 F2
Carolbrook Rd. IP2	14 D2
Carr St. IP4	5 D2
Castle Rd. IP1	7 E5
Catchpoles Way. IP3	16 C3
Cauldwell Av. IP4	13 E2
Cauldwell Hall Rd. IP4	13 E2
Cavan Rd. IP1	6 D4
Cavendish St. IP3	12 D4
Cecelia St. IP1	5 B3
Cecil Rd. IP1	5 A1
Cedar Av. IP5	18 C2
Cedar House. IP2	11 H6
Cedarcroft Rd. IP1	7 E4
Cemetery La. IP4	8 C6
Cemetery Rd. IP1	5 E1
Central Av. IP3	17 G3
Century Dri. IP5	19 C3
Chalon St. IP1	5 A3
Chamberlain Way. IP8	14 B1
Chancery Rd. IP1	5 A4
Chantry Grn. IP2	11 E6
Chapel Field. IP8	6 B4
Chapel La. IP8	14 B4
Charles St. IP1	5 B1
Charlton Av. IP1	7 F4
Chartwell Clo. IP4	13 F4
Chatsworth Cres. IP2	15 F1
Chatsworth Dri. IP4	18 A4
Chaucer Rd. IP1	7 F3
Chelsea Clo. IP1	7 F5
Chelsworth Av. IP4	8 B5
Cheltenham Av. IP1	7 G6
Chepstow Rd. IP1	7 G3
Cherry Blossom Clo. IP8	14 B1
Cherry La. IP4	13 F2
Cherry La Gdns. IP4	13 F2
Chesapeake Rd. IP3	16 C3
Chesham Rd. IP2	12 A5
Chessington Gdns. IP1	7 F6
Chesterfield Dri. IP1	7 E4
Chesterton Clo. IP2	15 E2
Chestnut Clo. IP5	9 H5
Chevallier St. IP1	11 G2
Chilton Rd. IP3	13 G4
Christchurch Ct. IP4	5 D1
Christchurch St. IP4	5 D1
Church Clo. IP5	18 D1
Church Cres. IP8	10 B3
Church Grn. IP8	6 B5
Church La. IP8	10 B2
Church La. IP6	8 C3
Churchill Av. IP4	13 F4
Civic Dri. IP1	5 A2
Clapgate La. IP3	16 C1
Clapgate Rd. IP3	16 C1
Clare Rd. IP4	8 D6
Clarence Rd. IP3	16 D2
Clarkson St. IP1	5 A1
Claude St. IP1	5 B1
Claverton Rd. IP4	18 A4
Claverton Way. IP4	13 H4
Clench Clo. IP4	5 E2
Cliff La. IP3	12 D6
Cliff Rd. IP3	12 C5
Clifford Rd. IP4	12 D3

Street	Ref
Clifton Way. IP2	14 C1
Clive Av. IP1	7 H4
Clovelly Clo. IP4	18 B4
Clover Clo. IP2	11 G5
Clump Field. IP2	15 E1
Cobbold Mews. IP4	5 D1
Cobbold St. IP4	5 D1
Cobden Pl. IP4	5 D2
Cobham Rd. IP3	13 G6
Cody Rd. IP3	17 F2
Colchester Rd. IP4	13 F1
Cole Ness Rd. IP3	16 D3
Coleridge Rd. IP1	7 F3
College St. IP4	5 C4
Collingwood Av. IP3	13 G6
Collinsons. IP2	11 E3
Coltsfoot Rd. IP2	11 F5
Columbia Av. IP5	18 C2
Columbine Gdns. IP2	11 F4
Commercial Rd. IP1	5 A4
Congreve Rd. IP1	7 G4
Coniston Rd. IP3	16 D1
Coniston Sq E. IP3	17 E1
Coniston Sq W. IP3	16 D1
Connaught Rd. IP1	6 D5
Constable Rd. IP4	12 C2
Constantine Rd. IP1	11 H4
Constitution Hill. IP1	7 H6
Conway Clo. IP2	15 G1
Cooks Clo. IP5	19 C2
Coopers Rd. IP5	19 F3
Copleston Rd. IP4	13 F3
Copperfield Rd. IP2	11 F4
Coprolite St. IP1	5 E4
Copswood Clo. IP5	19 D2
Coral Dri. IP1	6 D6
Corder Rd. IP4	12 C1
Corn Hill. IP1	5 B2
Cornflower Clo. IP2	11 F5
Coronation Rd. IP4	13 F4
Corporation Av. IP2	15 F3
Corton Rd. IP3	16 D2
Cotman Rd. IP3	16 C2
Cotswold Av. IP1	7 G6
Cottingham Rd. IP8	14 B2
Cowell St. IP2	12 B6
Cowper St. IP4	13 F3
Cowslip Clo. IP2	11 F4
Cox La. IP4	5 D2
Coytes Gdns. IP1	5 B2
Crabbe St. IP4	13 F3
Cranborne Chase. IP4	8 D5
Cranwell Cres. IP3	17 E2
Cranwell Gro. IP5	19 A2
Crawford La. IP4	19 A2
Crescent Rd. IP1	5 A2
Cresswell Ct. IP5	19 F4
Crocus Clo. IP2	11 F5
Croft St. IP2	12 B5
Crofton Clo. IP4	13 G2
Crofton Rd. IP4	13 G2
Cromarty Rd. IP4	9 E6
Cromer Rd. IP1	7 E6
Crompton Rd. IP2	11 F2
Cromwell Sq. IP1	5 B3
Crossley Gdns. IP1	6 C5
Crown St. IP1	5 B1
Crownland Clo. IP2	15 F1
Cuckfield Av. IP3	18 A6
Cullingham Rd. IP1	11 G3
Cumberland St. IP1	11 H2
Curlew Rd. IP2	11 E5
Curriers La. IP1	5 B2
Curtiss Clo. IP8	14 C2
Cutler St. IP1	5 B3
Daffodil Clo. IP2	11 F5
Daimler Rd. IP1	6 C5
Dale Hall La. IP1	7 G4
Dales Rd. IP1	7 F6
Dales View Rd. IP1	7 F6
Dalton Rd. IP1	5 A2
Dandalan Clo. IP1	11 E1
Darwin Rd. IP4	13 E4
Daunby Clo. IP2	10 D3
Davey Clo. IP3	16 C2
Dawnbrook Clo. IP2	14 D2
Dawson Drift. IP5	19 A2
Deben Av. IP5	19 D1
Deben Rd. IP1	7 E6

Deben Valley Dri. IP5 19 B3
Defoe Rd. IP1 7 F3
Demesne Gdns. IP5 19 E2
Denham Ct. IP5 19 E4
Denton Clo. IP2 14 C1
Derby Clo. IP4 13 E4
Derby Rd. IP3 13 E4
Dereham Av. IP3 12 D6
Derwent Rd. IP3 13 E6
Devlin Rd. IP8 14 B2
Devonshire Rd. IP3 12 D4
Dewar La. IP5 19 B2
Dial La. IP1 5 C2
Diamond Clo. IP1 6 D6
Dickens Rd. IP2 11 F3
Dickinson Ter. IP5 19 B2
Didsbury Clo. IP2 14 C1
Digby Clo. IP5 19 E4
Digby Rd. IP4 13 G2
Dillwyn St. IP1 11 H3
Dillwyn St West. IP1 11 H3
Ditchingham Gro. IP5 18 B3
Dobbs Drift. IP5 19 D2
Dobbs Gate. IP5 19 D2
Dobbs La. IP5 19 D1
Dock St. IP2 5 C4
Doctor Watsons La. IP5 18 D1
Dodson Vale. IP5 19 A3
Dogs Head St. IP4 5 C3
Dogwood Clo. IP3 17 G1
Dombey Rd. IP2 11 F4
Donegal Rd. IP1 6 D4
Dorchester Rd. IP3 13 H6
Dorset Clo. IP4 8 C5
Dove Clo. IP4 5 E2
Dover Rd. IP3 13 F5
Downing Clo. IP2 15 E1
Downside Clo. IP2 15 E3
Drake Av. IP3 13 F6
Drake Sq. IP3 13 F6
Dryden Rd. IP1 7 G4
Duckamere. IP8 6 A5
Duke St. IP3 5 E4
Dumbarton Rd. IP4 9 F6
Dumfries Rd. IP4 9 F6
Dunlin Rd. IP2 14 D1
Dunlop Rd. IP2 11 F3
Durrant Vw. IP5 19 D2
Dykes St. IP1 5 B1

Eagle St. IP4 5 D3
Eagle Way. IP5 19 E3
East Lawn. IP4 13 G1
Eastern Clo. IP4 18 C5
Eastgate. IP4 5 D2
Eccles Rd. IP2 14 C1
Eden Rd. IP4 13 F4
Edgeworth Rd. IP2 14 D1
Edmonton Clo. IP5 18 D2
Edmonton Rd. IP5 18 C1
Edward Clo. IP1 11 F1
Egglestone Clo. IP2 15 E2
Ellenbrook Rd. IP2 14 C2
Elliott St. IP1 11 H3
Elm Rd. IP5 18 B1
Elm St. IP1 5 A2
Elmcroft Rd. IP1 7 F5
Elmers La. IP5 19 B3
Elmhurst Dri. IP3 13 E6
Elsmere Rd. IP1 8 A6
Elton Park. IP2 11 E3
Ely Rd. IP4 8 D5
Emerald Clo. IP5 19 A2
Emlen St. IP1 11 H3
Emmanuel Clo. IP2 11 G6
Epsom Dri. IP1 7 G3
Ernleigh Rd. IP4 13 F3
Essex Way. IP3 17 G2
Europa Way. IP1 10 D1
Eustace Rd. IP1 11 F1
Euston Av. IP4 18 B3
Evabrook Clo. IP2 14 D2
Everton Cres. IP1 7 F5
Evesham Clo. IP2 15 F1
Exeter Rd. IP3 13 F5

Fairbairn Av. IP5 19 B2
Fairfield Rd. IP3 16 D1
Fairlight Clo. IP4 9 E5
Falcon St. IP1 5 C3
Falmouth Clo. IP5 18 D3
Faraday Rd. IP4 13 E4
Farriers Clo. IP5 19 F2
Farthing Rd. IP1 10 D1
Fawley Clo. IP4 13 G1
Felaw St. IP2 12 B5

Felix Clo. IP5 18 D2
Felix Rd. IP3 17 E1
Felix Sq. IP3 17 E2
Felixstowe Rd, Martlesham Heath. IP5 19 F1
Felixstowe Rd, Priory Heath. IP3 17 F1
Felixstowe Rd, Rose Hill. IP3 13 E5
Fellbrigg Av. IP5 18 B3
Fentons Way. IP5 19 A2
Ferguson Way. IP5 19 A2
Fernhayes Clo. IP2 15 F1
Field Fullers. IP6 8 C2
Fife Rd. IP4 9 F6
Finbars Walk. IP4 12 D3
Finborough Clo. IP4 18 B3
Finchley Rd. IP4 5 E1
Fircroft Rd. IP1 7 G3
Firefly Way. IP3 17 E3
Firtree Rd. IP8 14 B1
Fishbane Clo. IP3 16 D3
Fisks La. IP1 6 D3
Fitzgerald Rd. IP8 6 A6
Fitzmaurice Rd. IP3 13 F6
Fitzroy St. IP1 5 C1
Fitzwilliam Clo. IP2 15 E1
Fletcher Rd. IP3 16 C3
Fletchers La. IP5 19 C2
Flindell Dri. IP8 6 A4
Flint Clo. IP2 15 G1
Foden Av. IP1 6 C5
Fonnereau Rd. IP1 5 B1
Fordham Pl. IP4 18 B4
Fore Hamlet. IP3 5 F4
Fore St. IP4 5 E4
Forest La. IP5 19 E3
Forester Clo. IP8 14 D3
Forfar Clo. IP4 9 E6
Foundation St. IP4 5 C4
Foundry La. IP4 5 C4
Fountains Rd. IP2 15 E2
Fox Lea. IP5 19 C2
Foxburrow Rd. IP3 17 H2
Foxglove Cres. IP3 17 G2
Foxhall Rd. IP3 12 D4
Foxtail Rd. IP3 17 G3
Foxwood Cres. IP4 18 B4
Frampton Rd. IP3 16 D3
Francis Clo. IP5 19 C2
Franciscan Way. IP1 5 B3
Franklin Rd. IP3 13 F6
Fraser Rd, Bramford. IP8 6 B4
Fraser Rd, Ipswich. IP1 11 G2
Freehold Rd. IP4 13 E3
Freston Hill. IP9 16 B6
Friars Bridge Rd. IP1 5 A3
Friars St. IP1 5 B3
Friends Walk. IP5 19 C2
Fritillary Clo. IP8 14 D3
Fritton Clo. IP2 15 F2
Frobisher Rd. IP3 16 B2
Front Rd. IP3 17 G3
Fuchsia La. IP4 13 E4
Furness Clo. IP2 15 E3

Gainsborough La. IP3 16 C3
Gainsborough Rd. IP4 12 C1
Galway Av. IP1 6 D6
Gannet Rd. IP2 11 E6
Garrick Way. IP1 7 F4
Gatacre Rd. IP1 11 G2
Gatekeeper Clo. IP8 14 D3
Gaye St. IP1 11 H2
Gayfer Av. IP5 19 D2
Geneva Rd. IP1 5 A1
George Frost Clo. IP4 12 C1
Geralds Av. IP4 13 E4
Gibbons St. IP1 11 G3
Gifford Pl. IP4 18 C3
Gippeswyk Av. IP2 11 H5
Gippeswyk Rd. IP2 11 H5
Gipping Way, Bramford. IP8 6 B5
Gipping Way, Sproughton. IP8 10 C3
Gippingstone Rd. IP8 6 A5
Girton Way. IP2 15 E2
Gladstone Rd. IP3 12 D4
Glamorgan Rd. IP2 15 F2
Glanville Pl. IP5 18 D3
Glastonbury Clo. IP2 15 E2
Glebe Clo. IP8 10 C3
Glemham Dri. IP4 18 B4

Glenavon Rd. IP4 13 H2
Glencoe Rd. IP4 9 F6
Gleneagles Cres. IP4 13 H4
Gloster Rd. IP5 19 F2
Gloucester Rd. IP3 16 D1
Godbold Clo. IP5 19 B3
Goddard Rd. IP1 6 C3
Goddard Rd East. IP1 6 D4
Goldcrest Rd. IP2 10 D6
Goldsmith Rd. IP1 7 E3
Goodall Ter. IP5 19 D2
Goodwood Clo. IP1 7 G2
Gordon Rd. IP4 13 E2
Goring Rd. IP4 13 G2
Gorse Rd. IP3 17 E1
Gorsehayes. IP2 11 H6
Gostling Pl. IP5 19 C2
Gower St. IP1 5 C4
Gowers Clo. IP5 19 C3
Grafton Way. IP1 5 B4
Graham Av. IP1 11 H1
Graham Rd. IP1 11 H1
Grange Clo. IP5 19 D2
Grange La. IP5 19 D2
Grange Rd. IP4 12 D3
Grantchester Pl. IP5 18 C1
Grantham Cres. IP2 11 H5
Granville St. IP1 11 H2
Grasmere Clo. IP3 16 D3
Grayling Rd. IP8 14 D3
Great Colman St. IP4 5 D2
Great Gipping St. IP1 5 A2
Great Whip St. IP2 5 C4
Grebe Clo. IP2 11 F6
Green Oak Glade. IP8 14 C3
Greenfinch Av. IP2 10 D6
Greenspire Gro. IP8 14 B1
Greenways Clo. IP1 12 A1
Greenwich Clo. IP3 16 B1
Greenwich Rd. IP3 16 B1
Gresley Gdns. IP2 12 B6
Gretna Gdns. IP4 9 E6
Grey Friars Rd. IP1 5 B3
Grimwade St. IP4 5 E3
Grosvenor Clo. IP4 8 C6
Grove Hill. IP8 14 B4
Grove La. IP4 5 F2
Grove Wk. IP8 14 C3
Gwendoline Clo. IP4 18 B4
Gymnasium St. IP1 5 A1

Hadleigh Rd. IP2 11 E3
Hale Clo. IP2 14 C1
Halesowen Clo. IP2 15 E3
Halford Ct. IP8 14 B1
Halifax Rd. IP2 15 G1
Hall Rd. IP5 19 D1
Halliwell Rd. IP4 13 F3
Halton Cres. IP3 17 E2
Hamilton Rd. IP3 13 F6
Hampton Rd. IP1 11 G1
Handford Rd. IP1 5 A2
Hanford Cut. IP1 11 G3
Hardwick Clo. IP4 18 A4
Hardy Cres. IP1 7 E3
Harebell Rd. IP2 11 F5
Harrier Clo. IP3 17 E2
Harrison Gro. IP5 19 A2
Harrow Clo. IP4 13 F4
Hartley St. IP2 12 B5
Hartree Way. IP5 19 C2
Harvesters Way. IP5 19 E3
Haskins Walk. IP5 19 C2
Haslemere Dri. IP4 5 F1
Hatfield Rd. IP3 13 E5
Haughley Dri. IP4 18 C3
Hawes St. IP2 12 B5
Hawke Rd. IP3 16 B2
Hawker Dri. IP5 19 F2
Hawthorn Dri. IP2 10 D6
Hayhill Rd. IP4 5 F1
Hayman Rd. IP3 16 C2
Haywards Field. IP5 19 B2
Hazel Dri. IP3 17 H2
Hazelcroft Rd. IP1 7 G4
Hazelnut Clo. IP5 9 H5
Hazlitt Rd. IP1 7 F3
Headingham Clo. IP2 15 F1
Heath Field Mews. IP5 19 D4
Heath La. IP4 13 H4
Heath Rd. IP4 13 G2
Heath View. IP5 18 D3
Heather Av. IP3 13 G6
Heather Clo. IP5 19 E4
Heathercroft Rd. IP1 7 F3
Heatherhayes. IP2 11 H6

Heathfield. IP5 19 D4
Heathlands Park. IP4 18 B5
Helena Rd. IP3 12 C5
Helston Clo. IP5 18 D2
Henderson Clo. IP8 6 A5
Hengrave Clo. IP2 15 F1
Henley Av. IP1 7 H3
Henley Ct. IP1 7 H6
Henley Rd. IP1 7 H3
Henniker Rd. IP1 6 C6
Henry Rd. IP3 16 D2
Henslow Rd. IP4 13 F4
Henstead Gdns. IP3 16 D1
Herbert Rd. IP5 19 C2
Heron Rd. IP2 11 F6
Hervey St. IP4 5 E1
Hexham Clo. IP2 15 F1
Heywood Clo. IP2 14 D2
Hibbard Rd. IP8 6 C4
High St, Ipswich. IP1 5 B1
High St, Sproughton. IP8 10 B2
High View Rd. IP1 6 D6
Highfield App. IP1 7 E5
Highfield Rd. IP1 7 E4
Hildabrook Rd. IP2 14 D2
Hill House Clo. IP3 12 D4
Hillary Clo. IP4 13 E4
Hillcrest App. IP8 6 B4
Hillside Cres. IP3 13 G6
Hilton Rd. IP3 17 E2
Hintlesham Clo. IP4 18 B4
Histon Clo. IP5 18 C2
Hockney Gdns. IP3 16 D3
Hogarth Rd. IP3 16 C2
Hogarth Sq. IP3 16 C2
Holbrook Rd. IP3 16 B2
Holcombe Cres. IP2 14 C1
Holden Clo. IP2 12 B6
Holkham Clo. IP4 18 B4
Holland Rd. IP4 13 E2
Holly Blue Clo. IP8 14 D3
Holly End. IP5 19 E3
Holly La, Belstead. IP8 14 B4
Holly La, Rushmere St Andrew. IP5 9 H5
Holly Rd, Ipswich. IP1 12 A2
Holly Rd, Kesgrave. IP5 18 B1
Hollycroft Clo. IP1 7 G3
Holyrood Clo. IP2 15 E2
Holywells Rd. IP3 12 C6
Homer Clo. IP1 7 F3
Honeysuckle Clo. IP2 11 F4
Hood Rd. IP3 16 B2
Horseman Ct. IP5 19 F2
Horsham Av. IP3 13 H6
Hossack Rd. IP3 16 D3
Houghton Pl. IP4 18 B4
Howard St. IP4 13 F2
Howards Way. IP5 19 C2
Howe Av. IP3 13 G6
Howlett Clo. IP5 19 C3
Humber Doucy La. IP4 8 E4
Hunter Rd. IP3 17 E2
Hunters Ride. IP5 19 F2
Hurdle Makers Hill. IP8 10 A5
Hurricane Pl. IP3 17 E2
Hutland Rd. IP3 13 E2
Hyde Park Cnr. IP1 5 B2
Hyntle Clo. IP2 11 E3

Ickworth Cres. IP4 18 B4
INDUSTRIAL & RETAIL:
Alstons Ct Business Centre. IP3 17 F2
Boss Hall Business Pk. IP1 11 E2
Brookside Business Pk. IP1 11 F3
Eastway Enterprise Centre. IP1 11 E2
Elton Park Business. Centre. IP2 11 E3
Euro Retail Pk. IP3 17 G2
Hadleigh Rd Ind Est. IP2 11 F2
Orwell Retail Pk. IP1 11 G3
Portmans Walk Ind Est. IP1 11 G3
Quadrangle Centre. IP3 17 F2
Raeburn Rd Ind Est. IP3
Ransomes Europark. IP3
Riverside Ind Park. IP2
Rutherford Centre. IP1
Sproughton Ind Est. IP1
Whitehouse Ind Est. IP1
Whitton Light Ind Est. IP1
Yale Business Pk. IP3
Innes End. IP8
Inverness Rd. IP4
Ipswich Eastern By-Pass. IP5
Ipswich Southern By-Pass. IP3
Ipswich Western By-Pass. IP2
Ireland Rd. IP3
Iris Clo. IP2
Irlam Rd. IP2
Ivry St. IP1

Jaguar Clo. IP1
Janebrook Rd. IP2
Jasmine Clo. IP2
Jeavons La. IP5
Jefferies Rd. IP4
Jewell View. IP5
Johnson Clo. IP2
June Av. IP1
Jupiter Rd. IP4

Karen Clo. IP1
Keats Cres. IP1
Kelly Rd. IP2
Kelvedon Dri. IP4
Kelvin Rd. IP1
Kemball St. IP4
Kempton Clo. IP1
Kempton Rd. IP1
Kennedy Clo. IP4
Kensington Rd. IP1
Kentwell Clo. IP4
Kenyon St. IP2
Kerry Av. IP1
Kestrel Rd. IP2
Kettlebaston Way. IP4
Key St. IP4
Khartoum Rd. IP4
Kildare Av. IP1
King Edward Rd. IP3
King St. IP1
Kingfisher Av. IP2
Kings Av. IP4
Kings Way. IP3
Kingsfield Av. IP1
Kingsgate Dri. IP4
Kingsley Clo. IP1
Kingston Rd. IP1
Kinross Rd. IP4
Kipling Rd. IP1
Kirby Clo. IP4
Kirby St. IP4
Kirkham Clo. IP2
Kitchener Rd. IP1
Kittiwake Clo. IP2
Knights La. IP5
Knightsdale Rd. IP1
Knutsford Clo. IP8

Laburnum Clo, Pinewood. IP8
Laburnum Clo, Purdis Farm. IP3
Laburnum Gdns. IP5
Lacey St. IP4
Lacon Rd. IP8
Ladywood Rd. IP4
Lagonda Dri. IP2
Lakeside Clo. IP2
Lakeside Rd. IP2
Lamberts La. IP5
Lambeth Clo. IP1
Lambourne Rd. IP1
Lanark Rd. IP4
Lancaster Dri. IP5
Lancaster Rd. IP4
Lancing Av. IP4
Landseer Clo. IP3
Landseer Rd. IP3

Street	Ref
rcost Way. IP2	15 F2
downe Rd. IP4	13 E3
ing Rd. IP2	10 D6
croft Clo. IP1	7 H3
croft Rd. IP1	7 G5
wood Clo. IP2	10 D4
ent Gro. IP5	19 C2
Rise. IP5	19 F3
ill Dri. IP5	18 B3
pur Rd. IP2	11 F5
e Av. IP4	13 G2
l Av. IP5	18 D2
lhayes. IP2	11 H6
nder Hill. IP2	11 F5
nham Rd. IP2	11 F3
ord Pl. IP4	18 B3
d. IP3	13 E6
att Dri. IP8	6 A5
ster Clo. IP2	15 E2
ton Rd. IP3	16 C3
ton Sq. IP3	16 C3
Rd. IP3	16 C3
old Gdns. IP4	13 F1
old Rd. IP4	13 F1
e Rd. IP3	17 F2
gton Rd. IP3	13 E5
s Clo. IP3	18 A6
Croft Clo. IP1	7 F3
rick Clo. IP1	6 D4
s Av. IP8	6 B4
tree Dri. IP3	17 G1
ln Clo. IP1	7 G3
ergh Rd. IP3	17 E2
sfarne Clo. IP2	15 F2
ey Rd. IP4	13 G2
ield Rd. IP1	7 G3
ide. IP5	19 E3
field. IP5	18 B2
field Gdns. IP5	18 B2
t Rd. IP2	11 E5
St. IP1	5 B2
Rd. IP1	7 E5
Croft St. IP2	12 B6
Gipping St. IP1	5 A2
s Cres. IP2	12 B5
s Av. IP1	5 C2
no Rd. IP3	13 F6
ard Ct. IP4	13 E2
on Rd. IP1	5 A1
Barn Ct. IP1	11 E1
St. IP4	5 E3
dale Clo. IP4	12 D2
ne Way. IP8	6 A4
Clo. IP1	6 C5
ofts Dri. IP1	6 C5
r Brook St. IP4	5 C3
r Dales	
w Rd. IP1	7 F6
r Orwell St. IP4	5 D3
r Rd. IP6	8 A1
r St. IP8	10 B2
y Gdns. IP3	16 D3
w Clo. IP1	7 G2
rth Av. IP3	13 H6
nis Vale. IP5	19 A3
Rd. IP2	11 F5
r Rd. IP2	12 A5
hurst Av. IP4	13 H3
Ct. IP5	19 C2
der Dri. IP3	17 E3
ulay Rd. IP1	7 F3
enzie Dri. IP5	18 D1
alene Clo. IP2	15 E1
ngley Cres. IP5	18 B3
ie Clo. IP8	14 B1
enhall App. IP2	12 A6
enhall Grn. IP2	15 G1
Rd. IP5	19 A1
s Corner. IP1	5 D2
rd Way. IP2	11 F6
whayes Clo. IP2	11 H6
esbury Clo. IP2	15 F2
ern Clo, sgrave. IP5	18 B2
ern Clo, e Hill. IP4	13 F5
hester Rd. IP2	14 C1
y Clo. IP4	13 F3
all Walk. IP5	19 C2
ington Clo. IP4	18 B3
r Rd, vich. IP4	8 B6
r Rd, Martlesham th. IP5	19 F2
field Av. IP1	7 E5
Maple Clo. IP2	11 G5
Marbled White Dri. IP8	14 D3
Margate Rd. IP3	13 G6
Marigold Av. IP2	11 F5
Marlborough Rd. IP4	13 E3
Marlow Rd. IP1	6 D5
Marshall Clo. IP5	19 A2
Martin Rd. IP2	12 A5
Martin Side. IP5	19 F2
Martinet Grn. IP3	17 E3
Maryon Rd. IP3	16 D3
Mather Way. IP2	12 B5
Matlock Clo. IP2	14 B1
Matson Rd. IP1	7 F6
Maudslay Rd. IP1	6 C5
Maybury Rd. IP3	17 E2
Maycroft Clo. IP1	7 G3
Mayfield La. IP5	19 E4
Mayfield Rd. IP4	13 G1
Mayfields. IP5	19 E4
Meadowside Gdns. IP4	18 B1
Meadowvale Clo. IP4	13 E1
Medway Rd. IP3	13 E6
Melbourne Rd. IP4	13 H2
Melford Clo. IP4	18 C4
Melplash Clo. IP3	18 A5
Melplash Rd. IP3	18 A5
Melrose Gdns. IP4	9 E6
Melville Rd. IP4	12 D4
Mendip Dri. IP5	18 B2
Mere Gdns. IP4	18 B5
Merrion Clo. IP2	14 B1
Mersey Rd. IP3	12 D6
Michigan Clo. IP5	18 D2
Middleton Clo. IP2	14 C1
Milden Rd. IP2	11 E4
Mildmay Rd. IP3	16 D2
Mill Field. IP8	6 B4
Mill La. IP8	6 B5
Mill Rd Dri. IP3	17 H2
Millenium Way. IP5	19 C3
Millfield Gdns. IP4	13 F2
Milner St. IP4	5 F2
Milnrow. IP2	14 B1
Milton St. IP4	13 F2
Mitford Clo. IP1	7 G3
Mitre Way. IP3	12 D5
Moat Farm Clo. IP4	12 D1
Moffat Av. IP4	9 E5
Monarch Way. IP8	14 C3
Monks Gate. IP8	10 B3
Monmouth Clo. IP2	15 G2
Montana Rd. IP5	18 D2
Montgomery Rd. IP2	15 G2
Monton Rise. IP2	14 C1
Moore Rd. IP1	7 F3
Moorfield Clo. IP5	19 B2
Morgan Dri. IP5	6 C5
Morland Rd. IP3	16 C3
Mornington Av. IP1	7 F6
Moss La. IP6	8 D3
Mottram Clo. IP2	14 C1
Mount Dri. IP3	17 H2
Mumford Rd. IP1	7 E6
Munnings Clo. IP3	16 D3
Murray Rd. IP3	13 E5
Murrills Rd. IP3	17 G2
Museum St. IP1	5 B2
Myrtle Rd. IP3	12 D5
Nacton Rd. IP3	13 E5
Nactons Cres. IP3	16 D1
Nansen Rd. IP3	17 E1
Nash Gdns. IP3	16 D3
Navarre St. IP1	5 C1
Neale St. IP1	5 C1
Neath Dri. IP2	15 F2
Nelson Rd. IP4	13 E2
Neptune Sq. IP4	5 E4
Netherwood Ct. IP5	19 E4
Netley Clo. IP2	15 E3
New Cardinal St. IP1	5 A4
New Cut East. IP3	5 C4
New Cut West. IP2	12 B5
Newark Clo. IP2	15 E2
Newbury Rd. IP4	13 F3
Newby Dri. IP4	18 B4
Newnham Ct. IP2	14 D2
Newquay Clo. IP5	18 C3
Newson St. IP1	11 H2
Newton Rd. IP3	13 E5
Newton St. IP1	5 E2
Nightingale Rd. IP3	16 D3
Nightingale Sq. IP3	16 D3
Nihill Gdns. IP4	12 D3
Nine Acres. IP2	11 E3
Norfolk Rd. IP4	5 E1
Norman Cres. IP3	16 D1
North Clo. IP4	8 B6
North Hill St. IP4	5 F1
North Lawn. IP4	13 G1
Northgate St. IP1	5 C2
Norwich Rd, Ipswich. IP1	5 A1
Norwich Rd, Whitton. IP1	7 E4
Nottidge Rd. IP4	12 D3
Oak Clo. IP4	18 B1
Oak Eggar Chase. IP8	14 C3
Oak Hill La. IP2	12 A5
Oak La. IP1	5 C2
Oaklee. IP2	15 F2
Oaksmere Gdns. IP2	15 F1
Oakstead Clo. IP4	13 E3
Oban St. IP1	11 H2
Old Cattle Market. IP4	5 C3
Old Foundary Rd. IP4	5 D2
Old Norwich Rd. IP1	6 D1
Oldfield Rd. IP8	14 B2
Olympus Clo. IP1	6 D4
Onehouse La. IP1	7 H5
Opal Av. IP1	6 D6
Orchard Gate. IP2	10 D4
Orchard Gro. IP5	18 C2
Orchard Rd. IP8	6 A5
Orchard St. IP4	5 E2
Orchid Clo. IP2	11 F5
Oregon Rd. IP5	18 D2
Orford St. IP1	5 A1
Orkney Rd. IP4	8 D6
Orwell Bridge. IP3	16 A4
Orwell Gdns. IP2	11 G6
Orwell Pl. IP4	5 D3
Orwell Rd. IP3	13 F4
Osborne Rd. IP3	13 E5
Oulton Rd. IP3	12 D6
Oxford Rd, Ipswich. IP4	5 F2
Oxford Rd, Kesgrave. IP5	18 C2
Packard Pl. IP8	6 B5
Packard Way. IP3	17 E1
Padstow Rd. IP5	18 C3
Page Gdns. IP5	19 D2
Paget Rd. IP1	11 H2
Palmcroft Clo. IP1	7 G4
Palmcroft Rd. IP1	7 G4
Palmerston Rd. IP4	5 F2
Paper Mill La. IP8	6 B1
Parade Rd. IP4	12 D2
Pardoe Clo. IP4	18 A4
Park Clo. IP5	19 E2
Park Nth. IP4	8 B6
Park Rd. IP1	12 B1
Park View Rd. IP1	7 G6
Parkers Pl. IP5	19 E2
Parkside Av. IP4	12 C2
Parliament Rd. IP4	13 F4
Parnell Clo. IP1	7 F3
Parnell Rd. IP1	7 F3
Parnham Pl. IP4	18 C3
Partridge Rd. IP2	11 E5
Patteson St. IP3	12 C5
Pauline St. IP2	12 B5
Pauls Rd. IP2	11 F4
Peacock Clo. IP8	14 B1
Peacock St. IP5	19 C2
Pearce Rd. IP3	13 E4
Pearcroft Rd. IP1	7 G4
Pearl Rd. IP1	6 D6
Pearse Way. IP3	17 G2
Pearson Rd. IP3	13 G4
Peel St. IP1	5 C1
Peel Yd. IP5	19 E1
Peewit Rd. IP2	10 D6
Pelican Clo. IP2	11 F6
Pembroke Clo. IP2	12 A6
Pendleton Rd. IP2	14 C2
Penny La. IP3	17 H2
Penny Royal Gdns. IP2	11 F4
Penryn Rd. IP5	18 C2
Penshurst Rd. IP3	13 H5
Penzance Rd. IP5	18 B3
Peppercorn Way. IP2	12 B6
Perkins Way. IP3	16 C2
Peterhouse Clo. IP2	15 E1
Pheasant Rd. IP2	11 E6
Philip Rd. IP2	12 A5
Phoenix Rd. IP4	13 F2
Pickwick Rd. IP2	11 F3
Picton Av. IP1	8 B6
Pigeons La. IP8	10 A6
Pilbroughs Walk. IP5	19 A2
Pimpernel Rd. IP2	11 F5
Pine Av. IP1	7 G6
Pine Bank. IP5	19 D3
Pine View Rd. IP1	7 G6
Pinecroft Rd. IP1	7 F5
Pinetree Clo. IP5	18 B2
Pinmill Clo. IP2	14 C2
Pintail Clo. IP	11 F6
Pitcairn Rd. IP1	11 F1
Platters Clo. IP3	16 D4
Playford La. IP5	9 H5
Playford Rd. IP4	18 A2
Pleasant Row. IP1	5 D3
Plough St. IP4	5 F4
Plover Rd. IP2	11 F6
Pond Clo. IP4	18 B4
Poole Clo. IP3	13 H6
Poplar La. IP8	10 B6
Poppy Clo. IP2	11 F4
Portal Av. IP5	19 E1
Porter Rd. IP3	17 H2
Portman Rd. IP1	5 A1
Portmans Walk. IP1	11 G4
Postmill Clo. IP4	12 D2
Pound La, Belstead. IP8	14 A4
Pound La, Bramford. IP8	6 A4
Powling Rd. IP3	13 E6
Preston Dri. IP1	7 F5
Pretyman Rd. IP3	13 F6
Primrose Hill. IP2	11 G5
Prince of Wales Dri. IP2	15 F1
Princedale Clo. IP1	7 F5
Princes St. IP1	5 A4
Princethorpe Rd. IP3	13 G5
Prittlewell Clo. IP2	15 E2
Prospect Rd. IP1	11 G2
Prospect St. IP1	11 G2
Providence La. IP1	11 G2
Providence St. IP1	5 B2
Purdis Farm La. IP3	17 H1
Purplett St. IP2	12 B5
Quadling Rd. IP1	5 B4
Quantock Clo. IP5	18 B2
Quebec Dri. IP5	18 D1
Queen St. IP1	5 C2
Queens Sq. IP3	16 D1
Queens Way. IP3	16 D1
Queensberry Rd. IP3	16 D2
Queenscliffe Rd. IP2	11 H5
Queensdale Clo. IP1	7 G5
Queensgate Dri. IP4	8 D6
Quentin Clo. IP1	11 F1
Quilter Dri. IP8	14 C2
Radcliffe Dri. IP2	14 C1
Raeburn Rd. IP3	16 C2
Raeburn Rd Sth. IP3	16 B3
Ramsey Rd. IP2	15 F2
Ramsgate Dri. IP3	13 F6
Ramsome Cres. IP3	13 F6
Randall Clo. IP5	19 C2
Rands Circus. IP3	17 E1
Rands Way. IP3	17 E1
Randwell Clo. IP4	13 F4
Ranelagh Rd. IP2	11 G4
Ransome Clo. IP8	10 B2
Ransome Cres. IP3	16 D1
Ransome Rd. IP3	13 F6
Ransomes Way. IP3	17 F3
Rapier St. IP2	12 B6
Ravens La. IP8	6 A5
Ravensfield Rd. IP1	7 E5
Ravenswood Av. IP3	17 E3
Ravenswood Way. IP3	17 E3
Rayleigh Rd. IP1	7 E5
Rayment Drift. IP5	19 A3
Reading Rd. IP4	13 F2
Rectory Rd. IP2	12 B5
Redan St. IP1	11 H2
Redgate La. IP9	15 H6
Redwing Clo. IP2	11 E6
Reeve Gdns. IP5	19 A2
Regent St. IP4	5 F2
Regina Clo. IP4	13 F4
Reigate Clo. IP3	13 G6
Rendlesham Rd. IP1	11 H2
Renfrew Rd. IP4	9 F5
Reynolds Av. IP3	16 C3
Reynolds Rd. IP3	16 C3
Richmond Rd. IP1	11 F1
Riley Clo. IP1	6 C5
Ringham Rd. IP4	13 E3
Risby Clo. IP4	13 F3
Ritabrook Rd. IP2	14 D2
Rivers St. IP4	12 D2
Riverside Rd. IP1	11 F2
Robin Dri. IP2	10 D6
Roebuck Rd. IP3	16 B2
Romney Rd. IP3	16 C3
Rope Walk. IP4	5 E3
Ropes Dri. IP5	19 A2
Rose La. IP1	5 C3
Rosebery Rd. IP4	12 D4
Rosecroft Rd. IP1	7 G4
Rosehill Cres. IP3	12 D5
Rosehill Rd. IP3	12 D5
Rosemary La. IP4	5 C3
Ross Rd. IP4	9 E6
Roundwood Rd. IP4	13 E1
Routh Av. IP3	17 H2
Rowan Clo. IP3	17 G1
Rowanhayes Clo. IP2	11 H6
Rowarth Av. IP5	19 A3
Roxburgh Rd. IP4	9 F5
Roy Av. IP3	13 G4
Roy Clo. IP5	18 D2
Royston Dri. IP2	14 D1
Rubens Rd. IP3	16 D2
Rudlands. IP8	14 B2
Rush Clo. IP4	18 B5
Rush Ct. IP5	19 C2
Rushbury Clo. IP4	13 F1
Rushmere Rd. IP4	13 E2
Rushmere St. IP5	9 G6
Ruskin Rd. IP4	13 E4
Russell Rd. IP1	5 A4
Rydal Walk. IP3	17 E2
Rye Clo. IP3	13 H5
Saddlers Pl. IP5	19 E2
St Agnes Way. IP5	18 C2
St Andrews Clo. IP4	13 H4
St Aubyns Rd. IP4	13 E3
St Augustine Rd. IP3	13 H5
St Augustines Gdns. IP3	13 G6
St Austell Clo. IP5	18 C2
St Catherines Ct. IP2	14 D2
St Clements Church La. IP4	5 E3
St Davids Rd. IP3	13 F6
St Edmunds Pl. IP1	12 A1
St Edmunds Rd. IP1	11 H1
St Georges St. IP1	5 B1
St Helens Church La. IP4	5 E2
St Helens St. IP4	5 D2
St Isidores. IP5	19 C2
St Ives Clo. IP5	18 C3
St Johns Ct. IP4	13 F3
St Johns Rd. IP4	13 E3
St Lawrence Grn. IP5	18 D1
St Lawrence St. IP1	5 C2
St Lawrence Way. IP5	18 D1
St Leonards Rd. IP3	13 F6
St Margarets Grn. IP4	5 D1
St Margarets Plain. IP4	5 C1
St Margarets St. IP4	5 D1
St Martins Ct. IP5	19 C2
St Marys Clo. IP8	6 B5
St Marys Way. IP6	8 C3
St Matthews Church La. IP1	5 A2
St Matthews Pl. IP1	5 A1
St Matthews St. IP1	5 A1
St Michaels Clo. IP5	18 C3
St Nicholas St. IP1	5 C3
St Olaves Rd. IP5	19 A2
St Osyth Clo. IP2	15 E3
St Peters St. IP1	5 C3
St Stephens Church La. IP1	5 C2
St Stephens La. IP1	5 C2
Salehurst Rd. IP3	18 A6
Salisbury Rd. IP3	13 E5
Sallows Clo. IP1	11 G2
Salt House St. IP4	5 D4
Samford Pl. IP8	10 B3
Samuel Ct. IP4	5 E1
Sandhurst Av. IP3	12 D5
Sandling Cres. IP4	18 B4
Sandown Clo. IP1	7 G3
Sandown Rd. IP1	7 G3
Sandpiper Rd. IP2	14 D1

Street	Ref
Sandpit Clo. IP4	18 B4
Sandringham Clo. IP2	15 E1
Sandy Hill La. IP3	16 B1
Sapling Pl. IP4	18 B4
Sawston Clo. IP2	15 F1
Schreiber Rd. IP4	13 F2
Scopes Rd. IP5	19 A2
Scott Rd. IP3	16 D2
Scrivener Dri. IP2	10 D6
Selkirk Rd. IP4	9 F6
Selwyn Clo. IP2	12 A5
Serpentine Rd. IP3	17 E1
Seven Cottages La. IP5	9 F5
Severn Rd. IP3	12 D6
Sewell Wontner Clo. IP5	19 A2
Seymour St. IP2	12 B5
Shackleton Rd. IP2	13 F6
Shackleton Sq. IP3	13 F6
Shaftesbury Sq. IP4	5 E3
Shafto Rd. IP1	6 D6
Shakespeare Rd. IP1	7 E3
Shamrock Av. IP1	11 F5
Shannon Rd. IP3	16 C3
Shelbourne Clo. IP5	19 B2
Sheldrake Dri. IP2	11 E6
Shelley St. IP2	12 B5
Shenley Rd. IP3	16 D2
Shenstone Dri. IP1	7 F3
Shepherd Dri. IP8	14 B1
Sheppards Way. IP5	19 B3
Sherborne Av. IP4	9 E5
Sherrington Rd. IP1	7 G6
Sherwood Fields. IP5	19 A2
Shetland Clo. IP4	9 E6
Ship La. IP8	6 B5
Ship Launch Rd. IP3	12 C5
Shire Hall Yard. IP1	5 D3
Shirley Clo. IP1	7 F4
Shortlands. IP8	14 C2
Shotley Clo. IP2	14 C1
Shrubland Av. IP1	7 E5
Shrubland Dri. IP4	18 B3
Sidegate Av. IP4	13 E1
Sidegate La, Ipswich. IP4	13 E2
Sidegate La, Rushmere St Andrew. IP4	8 D5
Sidegate Lane West. IP4	8 D6
Silent St. IP1	5 C3
Silverdale Clo. IP1	7 F6
Simpson Clo. IP3	16 B2
Sinclair Dri. IP2	12 B6
Sir Alf Ramsey Way. IP1	11 H4
Sirdar Rd. IP1	11 G2
Skipper Rd. IP8	14 D3
Skylark La. IP8	14 B1
Slade St. IP1	5 D3
Sleaford Clo. IP2	11 H5
Smart St. IP4	5 D3
Smiths Pl. IP5	19 C2
Snowdon Rd. IP2	15 G1
Soane St. IP4	5 D1
Somerset Rd. IP4	12 D1
Sorrel Clo. IP2	11 F5
Sorrell Walk. IP5	19 E3
South Clo. IP4	8 B6
South St. IP1	5 A1
Southgate Rd. IP8	14 B2
Speckled Wood Clo. IP8	14 C3
Speedwell Rd. IP2	11 F5
Spenser Rd. IP1	7 E3
Spinner Clo. IP1	10 D1
Spitfire Clo. IP3	17 E2
Spring Rd. IP4	12 D3
Springfield La. IP1	7 F6
Springhurst Clo. IP4	13 E3
Springland Clo. IP4	13 E3
Sprites La. IP2	10 D6
Sproughton Ct. IP8	10 B3
Sproughton Rd. IP1	10 C2
Squires La. IP5	19 E2
Stable Ct. IP5	19 E1
Stamford Clo. IP2	15 E3
Stammers Pl. IP5	19 C2
Stanley Av. IP3	13 E4
Star La. IP4	5 C4
Starfield Clo. IP4	13 F3
Statchway Clo. IP3	16 D4
Station Bri. IP1	5 A4
Station Rd. IP2	12 A5
Station St. IP2	12 B5
Steckford Clo. IP4	18 C3
Stella Maris. IP2	11 E3
Stephen Rd. IP5	19 D2
Stevenson Rd. IP1	11 H3
Stewart Young Gro. IP5	19 B2
Stoke Hall Rd. IP2	12 B5
Stoke Park Dri. IP2	15 E3
Stoke Quay. IP2	5 C4
Stoke St. IP2	5 C4
Stollery Clo. IP5	19 A3
Stone Lodge La. IP2	11 G6
Stone Lodge La West. IP2	11 F6
Stone Lodge Walk. IP2	11 H6
Stonechat Rd. IP2	10 D6
Stopford Ct. IP1	11 G2
Stradbroke Rd. IP4	13 E2
Stratford Rd. IP1	7 E4
Stuart Clo. IP4	12 D2
Stubbs Clo. IP3	16 C2
Sturdee Av. IP3	13 G6
Suffolk Rd. IP4	5 E1
Summerfield Clo. IP4	13 H1
Summerfield Ct. IP4	13 H1
Sunfield Clo. IP4	13 F3
Sunningdale Av. IP4	13 H4
Surbiton Rd. IP1	11 F1
Surrey Rd. IP1	11 G3
Swallow Rd. IP2	10 D6
Swallowtail Clo. IP8	14 D3
Swan Clo. IP5	19 F3
Swan Hill. IP8	10 B6
Swan La. IP6	8 C2
Swansea Av. IP2	15 G2
Swinburne Rd. IP1	7 E4
Swinton Clo. IP2	14 C2
Sycamore Clo. IP8	14 B2
Tacket St. IP4	5 C3
Tallboys Clo. IP5	19 A2
Talmash Gdns. IP2	11 G5
Tamarisk Rd. IP3	17 H2
Tasmania Rd. IP4	13 H3
Taunton Clo. IP1	7 G3
Tavern St. IP1	5 C2
Teal Clo. IP2	11 E5
Temple Rd. IP3	13 G5
Tenby Rd. IP2	15 G2
Tennyson Rd. IP4	13 E3
Tern Rd. IP2	11 F6
Terry Gdns. IP5	19 C3
Thackeray Rd. IP1	7 E3
Thanet Rd. IP4	13 F3
The Albany. IP4	8 C6
The Avenue. IP4	8 A6
The Beeches. IP4	12 D4
The Bretts. IP5	19 C2
The Chase. IP5	19 F2
The Chestnuts. IP2	14 C1
The Drift, Ipswich. IP4	13 E2
The Drift, Martlesham Heath. IP5	19 E2
The Drift, Priory Heath. IP3	17 F2
The Driftway. IP4	13 F3
The Fairways. IP4	18 A4
The Greens. IP4	18 B5
The Grindle. IP8	10 A2
The Grove. IP1	7 H5
The Grove. IP5	19 E2
The Havens. IP3	17 G4
The Lawns. IP4	13 G1
The Limes. IP5	9 H5
The Lloyds. IP5	19 A3
The Maples. IP4	18 B1
The Mills. IP4	18 A1
The Oaks. IP5	19 D3
The Paddocks. IP5	19 E1
The Pastures. IP4	18 B4
The Sandlings. IP3	17 G3
The Spinney. IP4	18 B5
The Strand. IP2	15 H3
The Street, Bramford. IP8	6 A4
The Street, Belstead. IP8	14 B5
The Street. IP9	15 F5
The Walk, Ipswich. IP1	5 C2
The Walk, Kesgrave. IP5	18 D1
The Whinneys. IP5	19 C2
The Willows. IP5	9 H5
The Woolnoughs. IP5	19 B3
Theberton Rd. IP3	16 D2
Thetford Rd. IP1	11 G2
Thirling Ct. IP5	19 E4
Thistle Clo. IP2	11 F5
Thompson Rd. IP1	7 E6
Thornbush La. IP8	10 A1
Thornhayes Clo. IP2	11 H6
Thornley Dri. IP4	13 G1
Through Jollys. IP5	19 C2
Thurleston La. IP1	7 F1
Tinabrook Rd. IP2	14 D2
Tintern Clo. IP2	15 F1
Tokio Rd. IP4	13 E3
Toller Rd. IP3	12 C6
Tolworth Rd. IP4	13 E3
Tomline Rd. IP3	13 E4
Tortoiseshell Clo. IP8	14 D3
Tovells Rd. IP4	13 E2
Tower Church Yard. IP1	5 C2
Tower Hill Rd. IP1	11 G2
Tower Ramparts. IP1	5 B2
Tower St. IP1	5 C2
Trafalgar Clo. IP4	13 E3
Tranmere Gro. IP1	7 E4
Trefoil Clo. IP2	11 F5
Trent Rd. IP3	13 E6
Trinity Clo. IP5	18 C2
Trinity St. IP3	12 D5
Troon Gdns. IP4	9 E6
Truro Cres. IP5	18 C3
Tuddenham Av. IP4	12 C2
Tuddenham La. IP5	9 F4
Tuddenham Rd. IP4	12 C2
Turin St. IP2	12 B5
Turner Gro. IP5	19 B2
Turner Rd. IP3	16 C3
Turret La. IP4	5 C3
Twelve Acre App. IP5	18 D2
Tyler St. IP2	12 B5
Tyrone Clo. IP1	6 D4
Ulster Av. IP1	6 D5
Union St. IP1	5 D2
Unity St. IP3	12 D5
Upland Rd. IP4	13 E3
Upper Barclay St. IP1	5 D2
Upper Brook St. IP1	5 C2
Upper Cavendish St. IP3	13 E4
Upper High St. IP1	5 B1
Upper Orwell St. IP1	5 D3
Upson Way. IP5	19 C2
Upton Clo. IP4	5 F2
Uxbridge Cres. IP3	17 F2
Valiant Way. IP5	19 E2
Valley Clo. IP1	8 A6
Valley Rd. IP1	7 G6
Valleyview Dri. IP4	18 C5
Van Dyck Rd. IP3	16 D3
Vaughan St. IP2	12 B5
Ventris Clo. IP2	11 E4
Vere Gdns. IP1	7 H5
Vermont Cres. IP4	12 C2
Vermont Rd. IP4	12 C2
Vernon St. IP2	5 C4
Vicarage Clo. IP8	6 B6
Vicarage La, Bramford. IP8	6 B5
Vicarage La, Wherstead. IP9	15.G6
Victoria St. IP1	11 G3
Victory Rd. IP4	13 F2
Vincent Clo. IP1	11 F1
Violet Clo. IP2	11 G5
Wades Gro. IP5	19 C3
Wadhurst Rd. IP3	13 H6
Wainwright Way. IP5	19 B2
Walker Clo. IP3	13 G4
Wallace Rd. IP1	11 F1
Wallers Gro. IP2	11 F4
Walnut Tree Clo. IP8	6 A5
Waltham Clo. IP2	15 F1
Ward Rd. IP8	14 B2
Wardley Clo. IP2	14 C2
Wareham Av. IP3	13 H5
Warren Chase. IP5	19 C2
Warren Heath Av. IP3	17 F1
Warren Heath Rd. IP3	17 F1
Warren La. IP5	19 E3
Warrington Rd. IP1	12 A1
Warwick Rd. IP4	5 F1
Waterford Rd. IP1	6 D5
Waterloo Rd. IP1	11 G2
Waterworks St. IP4	5 D3
Waveney Rd. IP1	11 E1
Weaver Clo. IP1	10 D1
Webb St. IP2	12 B5
Webbs Ct. IP5	19 A3
Wellesley Rd. IP4	12 D4
Wellington St. IP1	11 G2
Wells Clo. IP4	5 E2
Wentworth Dri. IP8	14 B1
Wesley Way. IP1	11 F1
West End Rd. IP1	11 G3
West Lawn. IP4	13 G1
West Rd. IP3	17 G3
Westbourne Rd. IP1	7 E5
Westbury Rd. IP4	13 F1
Westerfield Rd. IP4	12 B2
Western Clo. IP2	18 B5
Westgate St. IP1	5 B2
Westholme Rd. IP1	7 F6
Westlands. IP5	19 E3
Westminster Clo. IP4	13 F3
Westwood Av. IP1	11 G1
Wetherby Clo. IP1	7 G3
Wexford Rd. IP1	6 D5
Weymouth Rd. IP1	13 E3
Wharfedale Rd. IP1	7 G5
Wherry La. IP4	5 D4
Wherstead Rd. IP2	12 B6
Whinchat Clo. IP2	11 E6
Whinfield. IP5	19 E2
Whip St. IP2	12 B5
Whitby Rd. IP4	12 D1
White Elm St. IP3	12 D4
White House Rd. IP1	6 C4
Whitethorn Rd. IP3	17 H2
Whitland Clo. IP2	15 F3
Whittle Rd. IP2	11 F2
Whitton Church La. IP1	7 E3
Whitton La. IP1	6 D2
Whitton Leyer. IP8	6 C5
Whitworth Clo. IP2	14 C1
Wicklow Rd. IP1	6 D4
Widgeon Clo. IP2	11 F6
Wigmore Clo. IP2	15 E2
Wilberforce St. IP1	11 H2
Wilding Dri. IP5	19 B2
Wilding Rd. IP8	14 B2
Wilkes Ct. IP5	19 C3
William St. IP1	5 C1
Willoughby Rd. IP2	12 A5
Willowcroft Rd. IP1	7 F4
Wilmslow Dri. IP2	14 C1
Wilson Rd. IP8	14 B2
Wimborne Av. IP3	13 H5
Wimpole Clo. IP5	18 B3
Wincanton Clo. IP4	8 D5
Windiate Ct. IP5	19 B3
Winchester Way. IP2	15 E3
Windermere Clo. IP3	16 D3
Windrush Rd. IP5	19 A2
Windsor Rd. IP1	11 G2
Winfrith Rd. IP3	13 H5
Wingfield St. IP4	5 D3
Winston Av. IP4	13 G1
Withipoll St. IP4	5 D1
Wolsey St. IP1	5 B3
Wolton Rd. IP5	19 A2
Woodbridge Rd. IP4	5 D2
Woodcock Rd. IP2	14 D1
Woodhouse Sq. IP4	5 E3
Woodland Way. IP1	6 C2
Woodlark Clo. IP2	14 D2
Woodpecker Rd. IP2	11 E6
Woodrush Rd. IP3	17 G1
Woodspring Clo. IP2	15 F1
Woodstone Av. IP1	8 A6
Woodville Rd. IP4	12 D4
Woolards Clo. IP1	11 G3
Woolverstone Clo. IP2	14 C2
Worcester Rd. IP3	16 D3
Wordsworth Cres. IP1	7 E4
Worsley Clo. IP2	14 C1
Wren Av. IP2	11 E5
Wright La. IP5	19 B2
Wright Rd. IP3	17 E1
Wroxham Rd. IP3	12 D6
Wye Rd. IP3	13 E6
Wynterton Clo. IP3	16 D2
Wyvern Rd. IP3	17 E3
Yarmouth Rd. IP1	11 G3
Yew Ct. IP2	11 H6
Yew Tree Rise. IP8	14 B2
Yewtree Gro. IP5	18 B2
York Rd, Ipswich. IP3	13 E5
York Rd, Martlesham Heath. IP5	19 F4

Aisthorpe. IP9
Ash Gro. IP9
Barnfield. IP9
Boydlands. IP9
Brook La. IP9
Broom Way. IP9
Bushey Clo. IP9
Catesbray. IP9
Cedars La. IP9
Chalkners Clo. IP9
Chapel Clo. IP9
Coombers. IP9
Crotchets Clo. IP9
Days Grn. IP9
Days Rd. IP9
Dodmans. IP9
Elm La. IP9
Farthings Went. IP9
Friars. IP9
Garrods. IP9
Glebe End. IP9
Great Tuffs. IP9
Hawbridge. IP9
Homefield. IP9
Jermyns Clo. IP9
Letton Clo. IP9
Link Rd. IP9
Little Grove. IP9
Little Gulls. IP9
Little Tuffs. IP9
London Rd. IP9
Long Perry. IP9
Longfield Rd. IP9
Mill Clo. IP9
Mill Hill. IP9
Mowlands. IP9
Old Rectory Walk. IP9
Penn Clo. IP9
Penny Meadow. IP9
Peters Gro. IP9
Playfield Rd. IP9
Plough Rd. IP9
Pound La. IP9
Red La. IP9
Red Sleeve. IP9
Rembrow Rd. IP9
Round Ridge Rd. IP9
Rylands. IP9
Sawyers Clo. IP9
School Clo. IP9
Smithers Clo. IP9
Snowcroft. IP9
Stockmers End. IP9
Tawney Clo. IP9
The Old St. IP9
The Pightle. IP9
The Squirrels. IP9
The Street. IP9
Thorney Rd. IP9
Tollgate Rd. IP9
Two Acres. IP9
Whitehorse Rd. IP9
Winding Piece. IP9
Windmill Hill. IP9

Addison Way. IP6
Aspen Clo. IP6
Back La. IP6
Bacon Rd. IP6
Barham Church La. IP6
Blue Barn La. IP6
Bramford Rd. IP6
Chapel La. IP6
Chestnut Dri. IP6
Church La. IP6
Coopers Way. IP6
Drury Rd. IP6
Eddowes Rd. IP6
Edinburgh Gdns. IP6
Ely Rd. IP6
Exeter Rd. IP6
Fletchers Clo. IP6
Foresters Walk. IP6
Giles Ct. IP6
Gipping Rd. IP6
Glebe Way. IP6
Hazel Rise. IP6

nfield Dri. IP6   26 D2
d Dri. IP6   26 A1
INDUSTRIAL & RETAIL:
aydon Ind Est. IP6   26 B1
lee Clo. IP6   26 C2
tes Way. IP6   26 A1
fisher Dri. IP6   26 A1
y Rise. IP6   26 C1
caster Way. IP6   26 D2
el Dri. IP6   26 A1
el Way. IP6   26 D3
Kiln Clo. IP6   26 C3
oln Gdns. IP6   26 D1
ge La. IP6   26 B3
on Ct. IP6   26 C1
dleton Rd. IP6   26 D1
La. IP6   26 A1
ers Ct. IP6   26 C2
gan Ct. IP6   26 C3
berry Gdns. IP6   26 A1
ell Rise. IP6   26 C3
wich Rd. IP6   26 C1
Ipswich Rd. IP6   26 C3
Papermill La. IP6   26 C3
Rectory Clo. IP6   26 C1
ard Gro. IP6   26 C3
ermill La. IP6   26 C3
ipps Rd. IP6   26 C1
mers Dell. IP6   26 A1
ar Clo. IP6   26 D3
its Field. IP6   26 C2
eters Av. IP6   26 C2
eters Clo. IP6   26 C2
eters Ct. IP6   26 C2
ion Rd. IP6   26 C2
Beeches. IP6   26 C3
Pines. IP6   26 C2
Slade. IP6   26 D1
rnhill Rd. IP6   26 D1
wright Gdns. IP6   26 A1
vers Way. IP6   26 C1
ow Clo. IP6   26 D3
chester Gdns. IP6   26 D1
lner Clo. IP6   26 C2
Cres. IP6   26 C2

FELIXSTOWE

stral Clo. IP11   C4
ington Rd. IP11   23 C5
ingham Mews. IP11   20 B3
andra Rd. IP11   20 C2
rew Clo. IP11   22 D2
e St. IP11   22 C2
ani Av. IP11   20 A4
ela Rd. IP11   20 D6
ot Dri. IP11   20 C2
ground Clo. IP11   23 B3
a Rd. IP11   20 D2
La. IP11   20 D3
on Rd. IP11   20 D5
field. IP11   20 B3
ns Clo. IP11   21 G2
on Rd. IP11   21 F4
Hill. IP11   21 F4
Rd. IP11   21 F4
dsey Clo. IP11   21 H1
ch Rd East. IP11   21 F4
ch Rd West. IP11   20 D6
ch Sta Rd. IP11   D3
con Field. IP11   20 C3
rice Av. IP11   21 E3
Hill. IP11   21 E5
ers Rd. IP11   21 F4
ops Clo. IP11   21 G2
eld Rd. IP11   20 A4
Barn Clo. IP11   23 B3
ord Way. IP11   20 A4
ord Ct. IP11   20 B5
kley Clo. IP11   20 B3
don Rd. IP11   20 A4
field Clo. IP11   20 B3
Kiln Clo. IP11   23 B3
kmakers Ct. IP11   23 A2
ge Rd. IP11   20 D4
htwell Clo. IP11   20 A4
kley Way. IP11   21 H1
k La. IP11   21 F3
k La. IP11   23 D2
herton Av. IP11   23 C4
vnlow Rd. IP11   21 E5
n Av. IP11   22 A2
gate Rd. IP11   20 D6

Burnham Clo. IP11   23 C5
Burwood Pl. IP11   23 C5
Buttermere Gro. IP11   21 H2
Cage La. IP11   20 C3
Cambridge Rd. IP11   21 F5
Candlet Gro. IP11   20 D3
Candlet Rd. IP11   20 C1
Capel Clo. IP11   23 B2
Capel Dri. IP11   20 B4
Capel Hall La. IP11   23 C2
Carol Clo. IP11   21 G3
Carr Rd. IP11   22 C4
Carriage Clo. IP11   23 C5
Castle Clo. IP11   21 H2
Cavendish Rd. IP11   20 D6
Cavendish Rd. IP11   23 A2
Charles Rd. IP11   22 D2
Chatsworth Cres. IP11   23 C6
Chaucer Rd. IP11   20 D5
Chelsworth Rd. IP11   20 B5
Chepstow Rd. IP11   20 D3
Chester Rd. IP11   20 D3
Chevalier Rd. IP11   21 E4
Childers Field. IP11   20 B3
Church La. IP11   23 B4
Church La, IP11   20 C2
Church Rd. IP11   21 G2
Cliff Rd. IP11   21 G3
Cloncurry Gdns. IP11   20 B5
Cobbold Rd. IP11   20 D4
Cold Store Rd. IP11   22 B4
College Grn. IP11   21 G3
Collimer Ct. IP11   20 C2
Colneis Rd. IP11   21 E2
Coniston Clo. IP11   21 H1
Constable Rd. IP11   21 F4
Convalescent Hill. IP11   21 E5
Conway Clo. IP11   21 G1
Cordys La. IP11   23 B6
Cornwall Rd. IP11   20 C3
Coronation Dri. IP11   22 C1
Cowley Rd. IP11   21 E4
Craig Clo. IP11   23 B2
Crescent Rd. IP11   21 E4
Cricket Hill Rd. IP11   20 B3
Cross St. IP11   20 C3
Crossgate Field. IP11   20 C3
Croutel Rd. IP11   21 E3
Crown St. IP11   20 C3
Crowswell Ct. IP11   23 B2
Cumberland Clo. IP11   21 H2
Dains Pl. IP11   23 C5
Darrell Rd. IP11   22 C4
Darsham Clo. IP11   20 B4
Dawson Ct. IP11   23 C4
Deacon Ct. IP11   21 H2
Deben Way. IP11   20 C5
Dellwood Av. IP11   21 E3
Devon Rd. IP11   20 D3
Dinsdale Clo. IP11   20 D5
Dock Rd. IP11   22 B4
Dooley Rd. IP11   22 B2
Dovedale. IP11   22 C2
Drovers Ct. IP   23 B4
Dukes Clo. IP11   21 H2
Dyke Rd. IP11   22 A2
Eagles Clo. IP11   20 D4
Earls Clo. IP11   21 G2
Eastcliff. IP11   21 H1
Eastland Ct. IP11   23 D5
Eaton Clo. IP11   23 C5
Eaton Gdns. IP11   22 D3
Elizabeth Way. IP11   22 C2
Elm Gdns. IP11   23 C5
Elmcroft La. IP11   21 G2
Ennerdale Clo. IP11   21 G2
Estuary Dri. IP11   21 G1
Euston Ct. IP11   20 A4
Exeter Rd. IP11   20 D3
Exmoor Rd. IP11   20 D2
Fagbury Rd. IP11   22 A1
Fairfield Rd. IP11   21 E3
Falcon St. IP11   20 C2
Farriers Went. IP11   23 D5
Faulkeners Way. IP11   23 C4
Feathers Field. IP11   20 B3
Felix Rd. IP11   21 E4
Felixstowe & Walton By-Pass. IP11   23 A1
Fen Meadow. IP11   23 C4
Ferndown Rd. IP11   21 F3
Ferry La. IP11   22 A2
Ferry La. IP11   20 B5
Ferry Rd. IP11   21 G1
Filling Point Rd. IP11   22 B3
Fleetwood Av. IP11   21 E3

Fleetwood Rd. IP11   21 E3
Foxgrove Ct. IP11   21 F3
Foxgrove Gdns. IP11   21 F3
Foxgrove La. IP11   21 F4
Friars Clo. IP11   21 H2
Gainsborough Rd. IP11   21 E4
Garden Field. IP11   20 C3
Garfield Clo. IP11   20 D5
Garfield Rd. IP11   20 D5
Garrison La. IP11   20 D5
Gaymers La. IP11   23 B4
Generals Mews. IP11   20 B3
Georgian Ct. IP11   20 D3
Glemsford Clo. IP11   20 B5
Gleneagles Clo. IP11   21 F2
Glenfield Av. IP11   21 E2
Golf Rd. IP11   21 G3
Gosford Way. IP11   21 G2
Goyfield Av. IP11   20 D4
Graham Rd. IP11   20 D3
Grange Clo. IP11   20 C3
Grange Farm Av. IP11   20 B4
Grange Rd. IP11   22 C2
Granville Rd. IP11   20 D5
Grasmere Av. IP11   21 H2
Great Field. IP11   23 C4
Grimstone La. IP11   23 A2
Grove Rd. IP11   21 E2
Gulpher Rd. IP11   20 C2
Gun La. IP11   23 A4
Hall Field. IP11   20 B3
Hall Pond Clo. IP11   20 B3
Hamilton Gdns. IP11   21 E5
Hamilton Rd. IP11   21 E4
Hamilton St. IP11   20 C3
Hauliers Rd. IP11   22 C3
Haven Clo. IP11   20 B4
Hawkes La. IP11   20 B2
Heath Ct. IP11   23 B3
Heathfields. IP11   23 A2
Heathgate Piece. IP11   23 C5
High Beach. IP11   21 F4
High Hall Clo. IP11   23 A2
High Rd. IP11   23 A2
High Rd East. IP11   21 E3
High Rd West. IP11   20 D3
High Row Field. IP11   21 G3
High St. IP11   20 C2
Highfield Rd. IP11   21 E4
Hintlesham Dri. IP11   20 B4
Hodgkinson Rd. IP11   22 A1
Holbrook Cres. IP11   20 B4
Holland Rd. IP11   20 D6
Hollybush Dri. IP11   21 G1
Hunters End. IP11   23 C5
Hyems La. IP11   21 F1
Ickworth Ct. IP11   20 B5
INDUSTRIAL & RETAIL:
Ferry Park Est. IP11   22 B1
Trinity Ind Est. IP11   22 B2
James Boden Clo. IP11   20 C3
Jasmine Clo. IP11   23 B2
Jubilee Clo. IP11   23 B3
Keepers La. IP11   23 B4
Kemsley Rd. IP11   20 D3
Kendal Grn. IP11   21 H2
Kentford Rd. IP11   20 B4
Kersey Rd. IP11   20 B5
Keswick Clo. IP11   21 G2
Kiln Field. IP11   20 B3
King St. IP11   20 C3
Kings Fleet Rd. IP11   20 C5
Kingsbury Rd. IP11   23 C5
Kirton Rd. IP11   23 B1
Knights Clo. IP11   21 G2
Lagos La. IP11   23 B4
Landguard Way. IP11   22 B5
Langdale Clo. IP11   21 H2
Langer Rd. IP11   22 D4
Langley Av. IP11   20 C4
Langstons. IP11   23 D5
Lansdowne Rd. IP11   21 F2
Larkhill Way. IP11   20 B3
Larks Way. IP11   22 C2
Lawn Way. IP11   20 C4
Leopold Rd. IP11   21 E5
Levington Rd. IP11   22 D3
Lidgate Clo. IP11   20 B4
Lincoln Ter. IP11   20 D5
Links Av. IP11   21 E2
Lodge Farm Dri. IP11   21 G3
Long Field. IP11   20 B3
Longcroft. IP11   20 C2
Looe Rd. IP11   21 F3
Lynwood Av. IP11   21 E3
Maidstone Rd. IP11   20 C3

Manning Rd. IP11   20 D6
Manor Rd. IP11   22 D4
Manor Rd. IP11   23 B5
Manor Ter. IP11   22 C5
Manwick Rd. IP11   20 C6
Marcus Rd. IP11   21 G3
Margaret St. IP11   20 C3
Marina Gdns. IP11   22 D3
Martello La. IP11   21 G3
Martello Pl. IP11   21 G3
Marys Cres. IP11   20 C2
Maybush La. IP11   21 G3
Mays Ct. IP11   20 D5
Meadow Clo. IP11   23 B2
Melford Way. IP11   20 B5
Mellis Ct. IP11   20 B3
Micklefield Mews. IP11   20 B3
Micklegate Rd. IP11   22 D3
Mill Clo, Felixstowe. IP11   20 B5
Mill Clo, Trimley St Martin. IP11   23 A2
Mill La, Felixstowe. IP11   20 B5
Mill La, Trimley St Martin. IP11   23 A2
Mill Pouch. IP11   23 C4
Monks Clo. IP11   21 G2
Montague Rd. IP11   21 E4
Nacton Rd. IP11   22 D3
Nayland Rd. IP11   20 A5
New Rd. IP11   23 C5
Newbourne Gdns. IP11   22 C2
Newry Av. IP11   20 D4
Nicholas Rd. IP11   20 A4
Norman Clo. IP11   21 G3
Northern Spine Rd. IP11   22 A2
Nursery Walk. IP11   20 D4
Oak Clo. IP11   20 C4
Old Kirton Rd. IP11   23 B2
Orford Rd. IP11   22 D3
Orwell Rd. IP11   20 D5
Otley Ct. IP11   20 B3
Oyster Bed Rd. IP11   22 A2
Park Av. IP11   21 F3
Park Ct. IP11   22 D2
Parker Av. IP11   20 A4
Parkeston Rd. IP11   20 B4
Parsonage Clo. IP11   20 B4
Penfold Rd. IP11   21 E4
Peewit Hill. IP11   22 C2
Philip Av. IP11   22 C2
Picketts Rd. IP11   21 F3
Platters Rd. IP11   22 D3
Plymouth Rd. IP11   20 D3
Polstead Ct. IP11   20 A5
Pond Clo. IP11   20 C3
Port of Felixstowe Rd. IP11   20 A4
Prestwick Av. IP11   21 F2
Pretyman Rd. IP11   22 D3
Princes Gdns. IP11   20 D4
Princes Rd. IP11   20 D5
Priory Rd. IP11   21 G3
Punchard Way. IP11   23 C5
Putley Rd. IP11   20 B4
Queen St. IP11   20 C2
Queens Rd. IP11   20 D5
Quilter Rd. IP11   21 F4
Quintons La. IP11   21 F2
Ranelagh Rd. IP11   21 E5
Recreation Clo. IP11   20 D2
Recreation La. IP11   20 D2
Red Hall Ct. IP11   21 G4
Red House Clo. IP11   23 B2
Reedland Way. IP11   20 B3
Rendlesham Rd. IP11   20 B3
Reynolds Clo. IP11   20 B3
Riby Rd. IP11   20 D5
Rogers Clo. IP11   20 D2
Roman Way. IP11   21 G2
Roseberry Rd. IP11   21 F4
Rosemary Av. IP11   21 F2
Runnacles Way. IP11   20 B3
Rush Meadow Way. IP11   21 H1
Russell Rd. IP11   20 D6
Rydal Av. IP11   21 H1
St Andrews Rd. IP11   21 E4
St Edmunds Rd. IP11   20 C6
St Georges Rd. IP11   21 G2
St Johns Ct. IP11   20 D5
St Martins Grn. IP11   23 B3
St Marys Clo. IP11   23 B5
Sandy Clo. IP11   23 B2

Saxon Clo. IP11   21 G2
*Schneider Clo, Sunderland Rd. IP11   22 C4
Sea Rd. IP11   22 D3
Seaton Rd. IP11   20 C3
Second Av. IP11   23 B5
Selvale Way. IP11   20 C4
Shotley Clo. IP11   20 B4
Shrubbery Clo. IP11   20 D4
South Hill. IP11   20 D5
Southern Relief Rd. IP11   20 A4
Springfield Av. IP11   21 E3
Sprites End. IP11   23 D5
Spriteshall La. IP11   23 D5
Stanley Rd. IP11   21 E5
Station Rd. IP11   23 C5
Stennetts Clo. IP11   23 B5
Stonegrove Rd. IP11   22 B4
Stour Av. IP11   20 C5
Stuart Clo. IP11   21 H2
Sub-Station Rd. IP11   22 C3
Sudbourne Rd. IP11   20 B3
Sudbury Rd. IP11   20 A5
Sunderland Rd. IP11   22 C4
Sunningdale Dri. IP11   21 F2
Sunray Av. IP11   21 F3
Surrey Rd. IP11   20 D4
Swallow Clo. IP11   21 G1
Tacon Rd. IP11   22 D3
Tarn Hows Clo. IP11   21 G2
Taunton Rd. IP11   20 D3
The Avenue. IP11   23 B5
The Courts. IP11   21 F4
The Downs. IP11   20 B3
The Josselyns. IP11   23 C4
The Kempsters. IP11   23 D5
The Pines. IP11   21 H2
The Walk. IP11   20 C3
The Wheelwrights IP11   23 C4
Thirlmere Ct. IP11   21 H2
Thomas Av. IP11   23 C4
Thorn Way. IP11   20 C4
Thornley Rd. IP11   21 G4
Thurmans La. IP11   23 B4
Thurston Ct. IP11   20 A5
Tomline Rd. IP11   21 E4
Tower Rd. IP11   20 D5
Treetops. IP11   20 C2
Trinity Av. IP11   22 A1
Tylers Grn. IP11   23 C5
Tyndale Gdns. IP11   21 F3
Ullswater Av. IP11   21 H1
Undercliff Rd East. IP11   21 F4
Undercliff Rd West. IP11   20 D5
Upperfield Dri. IP11   21 F2
Valley Walk. IP11   20 C4
Vicarage Rd. IP11   20 B4
Victoria Rd. IP11   20 D5
Victoria St. IP11   21 E5
View Point Rd. IP11   22 B6
Wadgate Rd. IP11   20 C4
Walnut Clo. IP11   21 H1
Walton Av. IP11   22 A2
Waveney Rd. IP11   20 C5
Welbeck Clo. IP11   23 C6
Wentworth Dri. IP11   21 F2
Wesel Av. IP11   20 B4
Western Av. IP11   21 G2
Westleton Way. IP11   20 B4
Westmorland Rd. IP11   21 G2
Whinyard Way. IP11   21 H1
White Horse Mws. IP11   21 G2
Wickhambrook Ct. IP11   20 A4
William Booth Way. IP11   20 B3
Windermere Rd. IP11   21 G2
Winston Clo. IP11   20 B3
Wolsey Gdns. IP11   21 E5
Woodgates. IP11   20 B3
Wrens Park. IP11   21 H1
Yeoman Rd. IP11   20 B5
York Rd. IP11   21 E4

HADLEIGH

Alabaster Clo. IP7   4 C4
Aldham Mill Hill. IP7   4 B1
Aldham Rd. IP7   4 C2
Angel St. IP7   4 B3

Street	Ref.
Ann Beaumont Way. IP7	4 A2
Ansell Clo. IP7	4 C3
Aylward Clo. IP7	4 C5
Banks Clo. IP7	4 C4
Barnes Cl. IP7	4 C3
Bell Mews. IP7	4 C3
Benton St. IP7	4 B4
Boswell La. IP7	4 B2
Bourchier Clo. IP7	4 C4
Bradfield Av. IP7	4 B3
Bradfield Cres. IP7	4 C3
Brett Av. IP7	4 D2
Bridge St. IP7	4 A3
Buckenham Rd. IP7	4 D5
Calais St. IP7	4 B3
Canterbury Gdns. IP7	4 C3
Carders Clo. IP7	4 C5
Carlton Walk. IP7	4 C5
Castle La. IP7	4 A2
Castle Rise. IP7	4 A2
Castle Rd. IP7	4 A2
Church St. IP7	4 B4
Churchill Av. IP4	4 C2
Clopton Gdns. IP7	4 C4
Coram St. IP7	4 A3
Corks La. IP7	4 A3
Cottesford Clo. IP7	4 C4
Cranworth Rd. IP7	4 C5
Delf Clo. IP7	4 D2
Drapers Clo. IP7	4 C3
Duke St. IP7	4 B4
Dunn Clo. IP7	4 C4
Dunton Gro. IP7	4 C5
Dyer Ct. IP7	4 D5
Edwin Panks Rd. IP7	4 C4
Freeman Clo. IP7	4 B2
Friars Rd. IP7	4 A3
Frog Hall La. IP7	4 C3
Fullers Clo. IP7	4 C3
Gaell Cres. IP7	4 C4
Gallows Hill. IP7	4 A2
George St. IP7	4 B4
Glanville Rd. IP7	4 C5
Guthrum Rd. IP7	4 B4
Highlands Rd. IP7	4 C4
High St. IP7	4 B3
Holbecks La. IP7	4 A5
Hook La. IP7	4 C6
INDUSTRIAL & RETAIL:	
Lady Lane Ind Est. IP7	4 C2
Inkerman Clo. IP7	4 B3
Inkerman Ter. IP7	4 B3
Jordayne Rise. IP7	4 D4
Lady La. IP7	4 C3
Layham Rd. IP7	4 A6
Lister Rd. IP7	4 D4
Long Bessels. IP7	4 C3
Magdalen Rd. IP7	4 B3
Maltings Mews. IP7	4 B4
Market Pl. IP7	4 B4
Meadows Way. IP7	4 B3
Meriton Rise. IP7	4 D5
Muriel Clo. IP7	4 D3
New Cut. IP7	4 C3
Newhaven Way. IP7	4 D3
Pound La. IP7	4 B3
Pykeham Way. IP7	4 B3
Queen St. IP7	4 B4
Ramsey Rd. IP7	4 D2
Raven Way. IP7	4 C5
Red Hill Rd. IP7	4 C1
Rousies Clo. IP7	4 C4
Schoorl Clo. IP7	4 C4
Shearman Rd. IP7	4 D4
Silkmill Clo. IP7	4 B4
Spooners La. IP7	4 B3
Station Rd. IP7	4 C4
Stockton Clo. IP7	4 D5
Stone St. IP7	4 A1
Stonehouse Rd. IP7	4 C3
Tayler Clo. IP7	4 C4
Tayler Rd. IP7	4 C4
The Green. IP7	4 C3
The Square. IP7	4 C2
Threadneedle St. IP7	4 C3
Timperley Clo. IP7	4 C2
Timperley Rd. IP7	4 C2
Tinkers La. IP7	4 B4
Toppesfield Clo. IP7	4 B4
Tower Mill La. IP7	4 D3
Weavers Clo. IP7	4 C3
Wentworth Clo. IP7	4 D5
Wilson Rd. IP7	4 C4
Woodlands. IP7	4 A3
Woodthorpe Clo. IP7	4 D4
Woodthorpe Rd. IP7	4 C4
Woolner Clo. IP7	4 D4
Yeoman Cres. IP7	4 C4
Yeoman Way. IP7	4 C4

MARTLESHAM

Street	Ref.
Alban Sq. IP12	9 F2
Angela Clo. IP12	9 F3
Bealings Rd. IP12	9 E1
Blacktiles La. IP12	9 E2
Buckingham Clo. IP12	9 E2
Carol Av. IP12	9 E3
Chandos Ct. IP12	9 F3
Chandos Dri. IP12	9 E3
Crown Clo. IP12	9 F3
Felixstowe Rd. IP12	9 F3
Green La. IP12	9 F2
Holfen Clo. IP12	9 G2
Main Rd. IP12	9 E3
Martlesham By-Pass. IP12	9 E3
Martlesham Rd. IP12	9 E1
Mill Rd. IP12	9 F3
Nunn Clo. IP12	9 G2
Post Office La. IP12	9 G1
Private Rd. IP12	9 F2
Ravens Way. IP12	9 F3
Redwold Clo. IP12	9 G1
Sandy La. IP12	9 G1
School La. IP12	9 G2
Shaw Valley Rd. IP12	9 F2
The Street. IP12	9 G1
Three Stiles La. IP12	9 G2
Viking Clo. IP12	9 G2
Viking Heights. IP12	9 G2

WOODBRIDGE

Street	Ref.
Adams Walk. IP12	25 D5
Andersons Way. IP12	25 B7
Angel La. IP12	25 C5
Ash Clo. IP12	25 C7
Aspen Clo. IP12	25 D5
Balliol Clo. IP12	25 A7
Barton Rd. IP12	24 B4
Beech Way. IP12	25 C7
Beresford Dri. IP12	24 C4
Bilney Rd. IP12	25 A6
Birch Clo. IP12	25 C7
Blakes Clo. IP12	24 F3
*Borrett Pl, Flynn Rd. IP12	25 A7
Bredfield Rd. IP12	24 C3
Bredfield St. IP12	25 C5
Briarwood. IP12	25 A7
Bridgewood Rd. IP12	25 B6
Brook St. IP12	25 D6
Broomheath. IP12	25 B8
Bullards La. IP12	25 A6
Burkitt Rd. IP12	25 B5
Burrows Rd. IP12	24 F1
Bury Hill. IP12	24 C4
Bury Hill Clo. IP12	24 C4
Cages Way. IP12	24 E1
Calder Rd. IP12	24 F1
California. IP12	25 A7
Carthew Ct. IP12	25 C6
Castle St. IP12	25 C5
Catherine Rd. IP12	25 B5
Cemetery La. IP12	25 B6
Chapel St. IP12	25 C5
Cherry Tree Rd. IP12	25 C7
Christchurch Dri. IP12	25 A7
Church St. IP12	25 C6
Church View Clo. IP12	24 F3
Churchill Clo. IP12	25 A6
Churchman Clo. IP12	24 E3
Clare Av. IP12	25 A6
*Clayton Ct, Flynn Rd, UO12	25 A7
Clements Rd. IP12	24 F1
Cobbold Rd. IP12	24 B4
Colletts Walk. IP12	25 A5
Collingwood Rd. IP12	24 C4
Conach Rd. IP12	25 B5
Coppice Clo. IP12	25 D5
Crane Clo. IP12	25 A7
Crown Pl. IP12	25 D6
Cumberland Mews. IP12	25 C6
Cumberland St. IP12	25 C6
Daines La. IP12	24 E4
Deben Rd. IP12	25 D5
Deben Way. IP12	24 D4
Dock La. IP12	24 E4
Doric Pl. IP12	25 D6
Downing Clo. IP12	25 A6
Drybridge Hill. IP12	25 B6
Dukes Meadow. IP12	25 A8
Dukes Park. IP12	25 A8
Edwin Av. IP12	24 B4
Farlingayes. IP12	24 B4
Fayrefield Rd. IP12	24 E4
Fen Meadow Wk. IP12	25 B6
Fen Walk. IP12	25 C6
Fernhill Clo. IP12	24 D4
Fitzgerald Rd. IP12	25 C5
Fitzwilliam Clo. IP12	25 A6
Fynn Rd. IP12	25 A7
Garrod Appr. IP12	24 F1
Girton Clo. IP12	25 A7
Gladstone Rd. IP12	25 D5
Gobbitts Yd. IP12	25 D6
Godfreys Wood. IP12	24 C4
Gonville Clo. IP12	25 A6
Grange Ct. IP12	24 D4
Green Man Way. IP12	25 D5
Grey Friars. IP12	25 A7
Grove Ct. IP12	25 C3
Grove Gdns. IP12	25 B5
Grove Rd. IP12	25 A5
Grundisburgh Rd. IP12	25 A5
Hackney Rd. IP12	24 E4
Hall Farm Clo. IP12	24 E3
Hall Farm Rd. IP12	24 E3
Hamblin Rd. IP12	25 D6
Hasketon Rd. IP12	25 A5
Haugh La. IP12	24 B4
Haughgate Clo. IP12	24 C4
Hawthorn Pl. IP12	25 A5
Hilly Fields. IP12	25 B7
Hope Cres. IP12	24 D4
Ipswich Rd. IP12	25 A8
Jacobs Way. IP12	25 D6
Jews La. IP12	24 F1
Kings Clo. IP12	25 B6
Kings Way. IP12	25 E5
Kingston Farm Rd. IP12	25 C7
Kingston Rd. IP12	25 C7
Lachlan Grn. IP12	24 B4
Lady Margaret Gdns. IP12	25 A7
Leeks Hill. IP12	24 D4
Lime Kiln Quay Rd. IP12	25 D6
Little St John St. IP12	25 D6
Lockwood Clo. IP12	25 C5
Lodge Farm La. IP12	24 E2
Love La. IP12	25 D5
Magdalen Dri. IP12	25 A7
Manor Rd. IP13	24 A4
Manthorp Clo. IP12	24 E3
Market Hill. IP12	25 C6
Melton Grange Rd. IP12	24 D4
Melton Hill. IP12	25 D5
Melton Meadow Rd. IP12	25 D5
Melton Rd. IP12	25 E5
Mill La. IP12	25 D5
Mill View Clo. IP12	25 A6
Mistley Way. IP12	24 B4
Moorfield Rd. IP12	25 B5
Moors Way. IP12	25 A5
Morley Av. IP12	25 C7
Naunton Rd. IP12	25 A6
Naverne Mdws. IP12	25 C5
Nelson Way. IP12	24 C4
New Rd. IP12	24 C2
New St. IP12	25 C6
Newnham Av. IP12	25 A7
Norman Clo. IP12	24 D4
North Hill. IP12	25 C5
Old Barrack Rd. IP12	25 A7
Old Church Rd. IP13	24 F2
Orchard Clo. IP12	24 C4
Osier Clo. IP12	24 D4
Oxford Dri. IP12	25 A7
Pembroke Av. IP12	25 A6
Peterhouse Cres. IP12	25 A6
Pilots Way. IP12	25 B7
Pine Wood. IP12	25 A7
Portland Cres. IP12	25 B6
Prentices La. IP12	25 A5
Pytches Clo. IP12	25 [cut off]
Pytches Rd. IP12	25 [cut off]
Quay St. IP12	25 [cut off]
Quayside. IP12	25 [cut off]
Queens Av. IP12	25 [cut off]
Queens Head Hill. IP12	25 [cut off]
Ransom Rd. IP12	25 [cut off]
Riverview. IP12	24 [cut off]
Rixon Cres. IP12	24 [cut off]
Rock La. IP12	24 [cut off]
Rodney Ct. IP12	24 [cut off]
Saddlemakers La. IP12	24 [cut off]
St Andrews Clo. IP12	24 [cut off]
St Andrews Pl. IP12	24 [cut off]
St Annes Clo. IP12	25 [cut off]
St Audrys Pk Rd. IP12	24 [cut off]
St Audrys Rd. IP12	24 [cut off]
St Edmunds Clo. IP12	25 [cut off]
St Johns Hill. IP12	25 [cut off]
St Johns St. IP12	25 [cut off]
St Johns Ter. IP12	25 [cut off]
St Peters Clo. IP12	25 [cut off]
Sandy La. IP12	25 [cut off]
Saxons Way. IP12	24 [cut off]
Seckford Hall Rd. IP12	25 [cut off]
Seckford St. IP12	25 [cut off]
Simons Rd. IP12	24 [cut off]
Smithfield. IP12	24 [cut off]
South Clo. IP12	24 [cut off]
Station Rd, Melton. IP12	24 [cut off]
Station Rd, Woodbridge. IP12	25 [cut off]
Sun La. IP12	25 [cut off]
Sutton Clo. IP12	25 [cut off]
Tanyard Ct. IP12	25 [cut off]
Tennyson Clo. IP12	24 [cut off]
The Avenue. IP12	25 [cut off]
The Debenside. IP12	24 [cut off]
The Grove. IP12	25 [cut off]
The Sidings. IP12	24 [cut off]
The Street. IP12	24 [cut off]
The Thoroughfare. IP12	25 [cut off]
Theatre St. IP12	25 [cut off]
Through Duncans. IP12	25 [cut off]
Tide Mill Way. IP12	25 [cut off]
Trinity Clo. IP12	25 [cut off]
Turn La. IP12	25 [cut off]
Turner Gdns. IP12	25 [cut off]
Turnpike La. IP12	24 [cut off]
Upper Moorfield Rd. IP12	25 [cut off]
Valley Farm Rd. IP12	25 [cut off]
Victoria Rd. IP12	25 [cut off]
Warren Hill Rd. IP12	25 [cut off]
Warwick Av. IP12	25 [cut off]
Waterhead La. IP12	25 [cut off]
Westholme Clo. IP12	25 [cut off]
Wilderness La. IP12	25 [cut off]
Wilford Bridge Rd. IP12	25 [cut off]
Wilford Bridge Spur. IP12	24 [cut off]
Wilkinson Way. IP12	25 [cut off]
Wilmslow Av. IP12	25 [cut off]
Woods La. IP12	24 [cut off]
Woolnough Rd. IP12	24 [cut off]
Yarmouth Rd. IP12	24 [cut off]

Edition 415 E 04.